MAJOR EUROPEAN AUTHORS

RIMBAUD

A CRITICAL INTRODUCTION

BY THE SAME AUTHOR

Le Lyrisme de Rimbaud, Nizet, Paris, 1938.
Rimbaud l'enfant, Corti, Paris, 1948.
An Anthology of Modern French Poetry. From Baudelaire to the Present Day,
Blackwell, Oxford, 1952. Fourth edition, 1976.
Rimbaud, Bowes and Bowes, Cambridge, 1957.
Autour de Rimbaud, Klincksieck, Paris, 1967.
New French Poetry: an Anthology with Introduction and Notes, Blackwell,
Oxford, 1973.

RIMBAUD

A CRITICAL INTRODUCTION

C. A. HACKETT

Emeritus Professor of French
University of Southampton

CAMBRIDGE UNIVERSITY PRESS

Cambridge
London   New York   New Rochelle
Melbourne   Sydney

Published by the Press Syndicate of the University of Cambridge
The Pitt Building, Trumpington Street, Cambridge CB2 1RP
32 East 57th Street, New York, NY 10022, USA
296 Beaconsfield Parade, Middle Park, Melbourne 3206, Australia

First published 1981

Printed in Malta by
Interprint Ltd

British Library Cataloguing in Publication Data
Hackett, Cecil Arthur
Rimbaud. —(Major European authors).
1. Rimbaud, Arthur — Criticism and interpretation
I. Series
841'8 PQ2387.R5Z/ 80—40455
ISBN 0 521 22976 6 hard covers
ISBN 0 521 29756 7 paperback

To my wife, a critical reader

CONTENTS

GENERAL PREFACE TO THE SERIES

The Major European Authors series, as the name implies, considers the most important writers of the European literatures, most often giving a volume to each author, but occasionally treating a group or a genre. The basic assumption is that the general reader and the student will be able to find information on biography and literary history fairly easily elsewhere. What he will look for in this series is a single volume which gives a critical survey of the entire œuvre or the most important works. Authors of books in the series are asked to keep this general objective in mind: to write critical introductions which will help the reader to order his impressions of the works of art themselves; to assume little prior knowledge, and so far as possible either to quote in English or to translate quotations.

It is hoped that the series will help to keep the classics of European literature alive and active in the minds of present-day readers: both those reading for a formal literary examination, and those who in the original languages and in translation wish to keep in touch with the culture of Europe.

PREFACE

This brief study is the result of some forty years of thinking about Rimbaud's work, and of discussing it with students and colleagues. In that time, my assessment of the importance and value of the poetry has not changed in any fundamental way; but my interest has progressively moved from the unconscious motives and forces to the conscious use of words, a change of emphasis that has resulted in a still keener appreciation of the work, and in particular of the *Illuminations*.

The writings have been taken in their 'traditional order', which, for reasons touched on in the text and elaborated elsewhere, I have always considered to be more accurate than the 'new order', tempting though it may be to end on the climax of the *Illuminations*. But it is the poetry, not the chronology, that finally matters. For this reason, I have concentrated on the poems themselves, selecting for discussion those which offer a variety of difficulties and, where appropriate, quoting them in full. I have not, however, attempted to give detailed, exhaustive commentaries; but I have tried, without, I hope, being dogmatic or exclusive, to indicate useful approaches and possible interpretations.

The quotations of the poetry and prose writings (taken from the Pléiade edition, *Œuvres complètes*, ed. A. Adam, Paris, 1972) have been given in the original, with accompanying translations. For the renderings (marked 'R. L.') of complete poems and of the more extensive extracts I am indebted to Professor Roger Little; of these only one poem, 'Le Cœur volé', is in verse, an exception prompted by its strong rhythm and insistent repetitions. Quotations from other writers, as well as shorter passages from Rimbaud's work, have been translated by me. The bibliography is restricted to essential editions, and to those books and articles which, in my experience, are most likely to be helpful to the student and the general reader. Finally, the chronological table includes not only the main incidents in Rimbaud's life, but also a number of contemporary events, literary and historical, some of which influenced him directly, and others which contributed to the climate in which he lived and worked.

I wish to express my sincere thanks to the staff of the Cambridge University Press, and in particular to Mr Michael Black for his patience and his constructive criticism. My thanks are also due to Mrs Jill Halliday for her skilled work on the index, and to the Edinburgh University Press for their kind permission to publish (with slight modifications) the commentary on 'Aube', which appeared in *The Art of Criticism. Essays in French Literary Analysis*, ed. Peter H. Nurse, Edinburgh, 1969 (pp. 217—24).

C. A. H.

1

INTRODUCTION

Au lecteur, maintenant d'admirer, comme il convient, le poète : en n'oubliant jamais, au cours des feuillets que l'œuvre lue, si géniale soit-elle, sort d'un cerveau de seule ment quinze, seize, dix-sept, dix-huit ans d'âge réel.

The quotation is from the preface, written by Rimbaud's first biographer Paterne Berrichon, and Ernest Delahaye, to the Mercure de France edition of the *Œuvres de Jean-Arthur Rimbaud* (1898). Although naive and fallible as critics, these two editors have stressed an essential, if obvious, fact about the work, and they have indicated an approach which remains valid. As we read, it may not be necessary or desirable to have constantly in mind Rimbaud's age, but this does help to place the poems and the poet in a context, and in a perspective at once human and literary. Other examples of artists who have been precocious, a Gilbert, a Chatterton or a Mozart, for example, may come to mind, but the particular nature of Rimbaud's genius, its flowering, explosion and sudden extinction, still astonishes, especially when it is remembered that he wrote all his poetic work in a period of about six years from 1869 to 1875, between the ages of fifteen and (as we now believe) twenty-one.

Other writers have written about their childhood and adolescence, and among major figures one thinks of Flaubert, Stendhal, Renan, Proust, Gide, Dickens, James Joyce; but theirs is an adolescence recollected and reconstructed in the light of their maturity. Rimbaud is unique in that he was able to express the turbulence, the conflicts and the idealism of adolescence, as well as a whole range of emotional experience, both real and imagined, while he was actually living them: 'Jeunesse de cet être-ci : moi!', as he exclaims in the *Illuminations*. From the beginning, he showed an astonishing virtuosity and mastery of known poetic genres, and his later work announced many of the themes, devices and techniques to be found in modern French poetry, on which his influence has been decisive. His work continues to arouse a response in the most diversified readers, whatever their religious, political, philosophical, psychological or literary persuasion. Critics have sought to prove that he was a Catholic, an atheist, a Marxist, a Cabalist, a Symbolist, a Surrealist, and the father of Existentialism. They have compared him to, among others, Faust, Prometheus, Icarus, Peer Gynt, Adam, the Good Samaritan, John the Baptist, Job, Christopher Columbus, Leonardo da Vinci, Joan of Arc, St Francis, the two Saints Theresa, the four Evangelists, Ezekiel, Isaiah, the Messiah, Orestes, Satan, and God —a list which is a measure of the impact of his writing and his life.

His few years of intense creative activity came to an end with his abrupt renunciation of literature at the age of twenty-one. The suddenness with which he stopped writing, and the enigma of his subsequent literary silence, have become an integral part of the Rimbaud legend, provoking hundreds of books and articles and creating a myth that has tended to obscure the poetry itself, an ironical reaction to one who was himself a destroyer of myths. A salutary recall to the text, a plea to 'read Rimbaud', was made in 1952 by the French critic René Étiemble.[1] Over a period of twenty years he had corrected inaccuracies and exaggerations; exposed falsifications, whether unconscious or deliberate; dispelled legends and myths; chastised those who had indulged in dithyrambic praise; and reprimanded those who had built extravagant theories on statements taken out of their context. In particular, he attacked the partial interpretations of all those who, like the Catholics, Communists, and Surrealists, have made of Rimbaud an idol or a god. Étiemble's tenacious efforts have resulted in a 'demythification', and have redirected attention to the problems in the poems themselves, and so to the richness and vitality of the work. This approach is now challenged by new linguistic theories, which regard the poem as a self-sufficient system of signs having no reference to the external world or to the poet's inner world of lived experience. While welcoming the end of the Rimbaud cult and the myth of the poet as a god-like figure, one is increasingly aware of the dangers of a linguistic method which treats a poet as a mere 'producer of signs'. Such an approach has the merit of disregarding the irrelevancies of anecdote, and of eliminating the vagaries of a purely subjective criticism; but it also tends to eliminate the poet himself who, rarely mentioned by name, becomes a 'narrator', a *scripteur* or an *actant*. The conflicts expressed in Rimbaud's work are more than a battle of words, and his poems are more than rootless 'pieces of writing', with a meaning limited to the sum total of their signs and grammatical features.

2

A 'PROLOGUE' AND EARLY VERSE POEMS

The earliest known text is a prose story of about seven hundred and fifty words to which some editors have given the title 'Prologue' and others 'Le Rêve de l'enfant'.[1] It was written probably at the age of ten, when Rimbaud was a pupil at the Institution Rossat in Charleville; and it displays that facility in using language to express personal feelings and conflicts which was to become a typical feature of his entire work. The first part is a dream about his birth, the parents he would like to have had, and his brothers, of whom he sees himself as 'le plus aimé'. The second part, quoted below, consists of protestations and revolt against the teaching of Greek, Latin, history and geography, against examinations, school and authority. It ends with his determination to live as a *rentier*, on the margin of society:

> Pourquoi, me disais-je, apprendre du grec, du latin? Je ne le sais. Enfin on n'a pas besoin de cela! Que m'importe à moi que je sois reçu ... à quoi cela sert-il d'être reçu, rien, n'est-ce pas? Si pourtant on dit qu'on n'a une place que lorsqu'on est reçu. Moi, je ne veux pas de place, je serai rentier. Quand même on en voudrait une, pourquoi apprendre le latin; personne ne parle cette langue ...
>
> Pourquoi apprendre et de l'histoire et de la géographie? ...
>
> Que m'importe, moi qu'Alexandre ait été célèbre? Que m'importe ... Que sait-on si les latins ont existé? C'est peut-être quelque langue forgée; et quand même ils auraient existé, qu'ils me laissent rentier et conservent leur langue pour eux! Quel mal leur ai-je fait pour qu'ils me flanquent au supplice.
>
> Passons au grec ... cette sale langue n'est parlée par personne, personne au monde! ... Ah! saperlipotte de saper-

lipopette! sapristi moi je serai rentier; il ne fait pas si bon
de s'user les culottes sur les bancs . . . saperlipopettouille!

The egoism and the protest of a child of ten against what he
was later to call his 'sale éducation d'enfance' are perhaps not
unusual, although surprising from one who was himself a brilliant pupil, particularly in the classics. The rebellious attitude,
however, coupled with the assumption of innocence, expressed
here so naively and amusingly, are to become dominant themes
in the subsequent work; and the emphatic 'je' and 'moi' (not
mere narrative devices), like the series of staccato interroga-
tions and exclamations, are typical of Rimbaud's later style.

His first poem, 'Les Étrennes des orphelins', was also written
while he was still at school, and in parts it reads like a sequel
to his Latin verse composition, based on an elegy by J. Reboul
entitled 'L'Ange et l'enfant'. 'Les Étrennes des orphelins' is a
lengthy narrative poem consisting of five sections of alexandrines, and it was published on 2 January 1870 in *La Revue pour
tous*, a journal to which his mother was a subscriber. At first
sight it might appear to be little more than a competent technical
exercise, in some aspects derivative, but here, as in most of the
early verse poems, there are personal and original features. It is
significant that, in this first poem, Rimbaud should have taken
as his theme childhood, and the child's ambivalent relationship
to the mother; and that hints of other major themes, such as
time, and the contrast between dream and reality, should emerge
through the veil of sentimentality. The 'visions blanches', which
the orphans see in their dreams, are pointers to the visions which
the poet, in 'Les Poètes de sept ans', endeavours to force from
his own eyes; while the lighted 'foyer' announces its counterpart,
the 'foyer noir' of 'Veillées', which becomes the source of hallucinatory images. Rebellion, open or latent, is always present,
even in poems which seem to conform to orthodox forms and to
the opinions of the adult world. This long poem is Rimbaud's
first skirmish with accepted values; and it is clear from his ambiguous attitude that he is mocking the conventional sentimentality of the readers to whom his text was addressed:

> Votre cœur l'a compris: —ces enfants sont sans mère.
> Plus de mère au logis! — et le père est bien loin!...

'Les Étrennes des orphelins' was followed by some forty verse poems which editors have grouped together under the title *Poésies*. These were written between December 1869 and October 1871; and while some are derivative, none is a passive, docile imitation. They vary in theme, style and versification, and in them Rimbaud is exhibiting his talents and his mastery of various genres and stanza forms. He is observing, recording, and above all attacking, testing himself against the work of his predecessors and contemporaries, whom he uses less as models than as obstacles to be overcome. It was perhaps the ease with which he equalled and even surpassed them that led to his contempt for their poetry, and eventually to the rejection of his own.

Several poems, such as 'Soleil et chair', 'Bal des pendus', 'Le Forgeron', 'Vénus anadyomène' and 'Le Dormeur du val', are only partially derivative. In 'Soleil et chair', there are reminiscences of Hugo, Banville, Baudelaire, and also of Alfred de Musset, whom Rimbaud came to despise, calling him 'quatorze fois exécrable'; but the well-worn Romantic theme contrasting a mythical past of innocence and happiness with a present of ugliness and corruption is revitalised by Rimbaud's feelings about nature, man and God. 'Bal des pendus' reads like an exercise on Banville's 'Ballade des pendus', with reminiscences of Villon's ballades and Gautier's 'Bûchers et tombeaux'; but there is originality in the sheer gusto, in the physical, almost muscular, lyricism in which vowels and consonants clash together as they re-enact the 'grand bal des squelettes'. 'Le Forgeron', which derives in part from Michelet and Hugo, is animated by a spirit of revolt, and the blacksmith's gesture of defiance is Rimbaud's:

> Alors, de sa main large et superbe de crasse,
> Bien que le roi ventru suât, le Forgeron,
> Terrible, lui jeta le bonnet rouge au front!

'Vénus anadyomène', where Venus rises not as a goddess from the foam but as a woman, 'belle hideusement d'un ulcère à l'anus', from a zinc bath, may have been inspired by 'Les Antres malsains' by Albert Glatigny, a minor Parnassian, or, more probably, by Baudelaire's recommendation to turn ugliness itself to account. This experiment in crude realism is also a ferocious, if facile and exaggerated, attack on conventional ideas of art, beauty and woman. 'Le Dormeur du val', a much anthologised piece, awakens echoes of the second tercet of Baudelaire's sonnet 'La Cloche fêlée', of Leconte de Lisle's 'La Fontaine aux lianes', and more especially of lines in Hugo's 'Nox' ('Ils étaient là, sanglants, froids, la bouche entr'ouverte,/La face vers le ciel, blêmes dans l'herbe verte/Effroyables à voir dans leur tranquillité'). The shock image in the final line of Rimbaud's poem ('Tranquille. Il a deux trous rouges au côté droit') recalls Hugo again in the beginning of 'Souvenir de la nuit du 4' ('L'enfant avait reçu deux balles dans la tête'); but in Rimbaud's sonnet there is a freshness of vision, a tenderness in his attitude towards nature and the dead soldier, a sense of the waste and tragedy of war, which are personal and authentic.

At the same time as he was writing these 'exercises', and other less successful ones like 'Première soirée' and 'Les Reparties de Nina', he was making poems from the first-hand experience of an unusually alert and sensitive adolescent. Among these are 'Les Effarés', 'Au Cabaret-Vert', 'La Maline', 'Ma Bohème', and 'Les Chercheuses de poux', and a series of important poems which express exasperation, indignation and revolt. At first, his anger is directed against people and incidents in his provincial environment. In 'Les Douaniers', he takes as his subject the customs men who used to search him and his friend Ernest Delahaye for tobacco as they returned from expeditions into Belgium; and in 'Les Assis' he satirises venomously and grotesquely the municipal librarians who reluctantly left their seats to satisfy his voracious demands for books. But in 'À la musique' his target is the entire citizenry of Charleville, his 'ville natale . . . supérieurement idiote entre les petites villes de province', as he wrote in a letter to his school teacher Georges Izambard.

À LA MUSIQUE

Place de la gare, à Charleville.

Sur la place taillée en mesquines pelouses,
Square où tout est correct, les arbres et les fleurs,
Tous les bourgeois poussifs qu'étranglent les chaleurs
Portent, les jeudis soirs, leurs bêtises jalouses.

— L'orchestre militaire, au milieu du jardin,
Balance ses schakos dans la *Valse des fifres:*

—Autour, aux premiers rangs, parade le gandin;
Le notaire pend à ses breloques à chiffres:

Des rentiers à lorgnons soulignent tous les couacs:
Les gros bureaux bouffis traînent leurs grosses dames
Auprès desquelles vont, officieux cornacs,
Celles dont les volants ont des airs de réclames;

Sur les bancs verts, des clubs d'épiciers retraités
Qui tisonnent le sable avec leur canne à pomme,
Fort sérieusement discutent les traités,
Puis prisent en argent, et reprennent: En somme!...

Épatant sur son banc les rondeurs de ses reins,
Un bourgeois à boutons clairs, bedaine flamande,
Savoure son onnaing d'où le tabac par brins
Déborde —vous savez, c'est de la contrebande; —

Le long des gazons verts ricanent les voyous;
Et, rendus amoureux par le chant des trombones,
Très naïfs, et fumant des roses,[2] les pioupious
Caressent les bébés pour enjôler les bonnes...

—Moi, je suis, débraillé comme un étudiant
Sous les marronniers verts les alertes fillettes:
Elles le savent bien, et tournent en riant,
Vers moi, leurs yeux tout pleins de choses indiscrètes.

Je ne dis pas un mot: je regarde toujours
La chair de leurs cous blancs brodés de mèches folles:
Je suis, sous le corsage et les frêles atours,
Le dos divin après la courbe des épaules.

J'ai bientôt déniché la bottine, le bas...
— Je reconstruis les corps, brûlé de belles fièvres.
Elles me trouvent drôle et se parlent tout bas...
—Et mes désirs brutaux s'accrochent à leurs lèvres.[3]

The title is ironical. It is not a serious poem addressed to music, it is a satire on a military band with its 'valse des fifres', false notes, and the trombone's absurd song that inspires the soldiers with love. These amusing discords are in keeping with the observations on the strutting fop, the notary, the civil servants, the grocers, the overdressed women, the sneering ragamuffins, the simple-minded soldiers, the flirtatious nursemaids, all in the mean setting clearly identified in the subtitle. In the opening stanza the place, the actors and the time are given. The men, women and youth of Charleville are arranged in a logical, hierarchical order, and form concentric circles that radiate from the centre-piece, the military band, to Rimbaud, the cynical observer, who stands on the fringe of the crowd. The picture is animated and sharply defined; and with the utmost economy of words, an action, an external feature, a detail evokes and caricatures. Two adjectives, 'mesquines' and 'correct', satirise the setting; one verb, 'portent', conveys the actual weight and burden of the unchanging pomposity of the bourgeois; and 'parade' portrays the exhibitionism of the fop. Another verb, 'pend', is used to produce a highly original and as it were inverted image, wherein the notary himself is pictured as hanging from his watch-chain along with the trinkets and seals of his office, a brilliant single-line caricature, as in a drawing by Cruikshank or Daumier, of the bourgeois clinging to outward signs and prestige symbols. The poem concludes with a self-portrait of the artist who, by his appearance and dress, isolation and silence, thoughts and desires, is in every way opposed to the bourgeois he views with a keen satiric eye; and he too is summed up in one word — 'drôle'.[4] As in many of the early poems, Rimbaud's way of looking at things is realistic and physical; and the combination of lively details, witty images and individual portraits results in a dramatised period piece that is also an enduring social comment.

Several details in the poem suggest the influence of Glatigny's 'Promenade d'hiver'; but the main inspiration for this provincial tableau may have been one of Baudelaire's *Tableaux parisiens* — 'Les Petites Vieilles' — which also contains an ironic reference to military music. Rimbaud's poem lacks, of course, Baudelaire's insight; but it is the authentic expression of an adolescent's vision, at once self-centred, detached and cynical. The interest lies as much in how Rimbaud sees himself as in how he sees other people. His role and attitude in 'À la musique', where he sets himself in his habitual context on the margin of society, is natural and characteristic, and for this reason the poem offers an appropriate vantage point from which to survey the *Poésies*.

As his experience grew and his technical skill developed Rimbaud turned from provincial targets to attack fundamental

things: love and women ('Mes petites amoureuses'), social shams
and hypocrisies ('L'Homme juste'), poets and poetry ('Ce qu'on
dit au poète à propos de fleurs'), politicians ('Chant de guerre
parisien'), rulers ('L'Éclatante Victoire de Sarrebruck'), tyranny
('Rages de Césars') and war ('Le Mal'). But chiefly his virulent
energy was directed against everything connected with religion.
In 'Oraison du soir', a sonnet which contains violent contrasts
and images of unusual beauty, his evening prayer consists of
pissing heavenwards:

> Doux comme le Seigneur du cèdre et des hysopes,
> Je pisse vers les cieux bruns, très haut et très loin,
> Avec l'assentiment des grands héliotropes.

This adolescent pride in a bodily function, performed with the
solemnity of a religious act, expresses the contempt of the poet,
a neo-pagan votary of 'Soleil' and 'Chair', for the practices of
religion and for God himself, 'le Seigneur du cèdre et des hy-
sopes'. In other poems of this period, the priest, religion's earthly
representative, is ridiculed as a 'noir grotesque dont fermentent
les souliers' and caricatured in 'Accroupissements' as a scatolo-
gical creature gripping a chamber-pot and dreaming of love.
Worshippers are described as slobbering out 'la foi mendiante et
stupide'; and churches are dismissed in the sentence 'Vraiment,
c'est bête, ces églises des villages.' Christ himself is referred to
as the 'Pleureur des Oliviers' and the 'éternel voleur des énergies';
and God, indifferent to war, suffering and evil, as laughing 'aux
nappes damassées/des autels'.

At times, Rimbaud appears to delight in aggression for its
own sake; yet his attacks are never gratuitous. The very nature
and excess of his anger, disgust and violence imply an objective
that he later formulates as 'changer la vie' — an objective that
demanded more than words and that could never be achieved
through them alone.

3

POETIC THEORY

The defeat of France in 1871 in the Franco-Prussian war was not unwelcome to the anti-patriot Rimbaud; but the failure shortly afterwards of the popular uprising of the Commune, with whose aims he was in complete sympathy, was an overwhelming disappointment. It was against this background that he realised the inadequacy of his work as a poet and the impotence of his own verbal rebellion. A fundamentally new approach was needed, and he attempted to formulate his ideas about this in two letters, one dated 13 May 1871 to his school-teacher Georges Izambard, and the other, two days later, to his friend and fellow poet Paul Demeny. The Izambard letter announced new ideas about the poet and the *voyant*, subjective and objective poetry, the 'je' and the 'autre', and the poet's role in society. The much longer and more important letter to Demeny developed these theories, and it is this letter which has become known as the *Lettre du voyant*. Each letter contained examples of Rimbaud's own poetry, but whereas 'Le Cœur supplicié' (subsequently named 'Le Cœur volé') is added as a conclusion to Izambard's, the three poems sent to Demeny are an integral part of the letter.

The term *voyant* has a long history of changing usage and meaning, going back to the Old Testament. It had been used just before Rimbaud's time by several nineteenth-century writers whose works he knew well, among them Michelet, Hugo, Baudelaire, Gautier, Leconte de Lisle, and Balzac; and many of the ideas concerning the social function of art, the liberation of women, progress, justice and an ideal society had already been expressed by writers such as Proudhon, Saint-Simon, Fourier and, of course, Hugo. Rimbaud seized these ideas that had been in the air since the middle of the nineteenth century, gave them a personal emphasis, and co-ordinated them into a poetic creed. In this sense, there is nothing absolutely new in this famous letter. It is a statement of Rimbaud's excited discovery of ideas

about himself and society, and it constitutes his literary manifesto.

He starts by saying that he has decided to give Demeny 'une
heure de littérature nouvelle', and then quotes one of his own
poems, 'Chant de guerre parisien', a devastating attack on
authority and the glorification of war, and ironically referred
to as 'un psaume d'actualité'. In the middle of the letter, he
quotes a second 'psalm', 'Mes petites amoureuses', a sadistic
thrust at conventional ideas of love and beauty; and at the end,
a third 'pious song', 'Accroupissements', an obscene, savagely
anti-religious text. These three poems, which were composed a
few weeks before the letter was written, do not illustrate Rimbaud's ideas about the new poetry, that of the *voyant*. They are
examples of a 'new literature', and more particularly of what he
himself could do even with existing verse-forms. With a typically
ambiguous use of exclamation marks to express pleasure in his
achievement, and also ironic self-defence, he has written down
the margin, opposite each poem: 'Quelles rimes! ô! quelles
rimes!' According to him, stupid generations of versifiers (including Racine, 'le Divin Sot') — the dilettantes, hacks and civil
servants of literature — had produced nothing more than rhymed
prose, whereas he, a sixteen-year-old, had written verse poems
that were revolutionary in spirit, as well as in the use of un-
familiar terms and neologisms.

His ideas about *voyant* poetry are set within the framework
of a rapid survey of poetry from the Greeks to the Romantics
and Parnassians, and in the still wider context of an aspiration
towards the unknown, and a new form of life for all mankind.
Although several critics have seen in this perfunctory survey
keen and discerning judgement, it is neither a sound historical
account nor a balanced assessment. Many of Rimbaud's opinions
about particular writers, like his observations on progress and
social reform, had already been expressed by others. Sainte-
Beuve, despite his admiration for Racine's use of the alexandrine, had declared that he could see in it nothing more than 'la
vieille forme merveilleusement traitée'; and in 1870, a year
ahead of Rimbaud's letter, Lautréamont had asserted in his
Poésies: 'Depuis Racine, la poésie n'a pas progressé d'un milli-
mètre ... Pauvre Racine!' Baudelaire had earlier disposed of
Alfred de Musset in a few incisive phrases such as 'un paresseux

à effusions gracieuses' and 'ce maître des gandins' which, like Lautréamont's formula 'Le Gandin-Sans-Chemise-Intellectuelle', are far more effective than the long rhetorical passage in the *Lettre du voyant*.

Rimbaud was likewise as uncritical and extreme in his praise as in his denigration (who today would call Albert Mérat a *voyant*?). He judges all poets by one criterion: the extent to which they had been *voyant*, that is, by the newness and purity of their vision and its expression. While Musset is condemned because he had been 'lazy' and had 'closed his eyes', other 'first Romantics', like Lamartine and Hugo, were *voyants*, but unconsciously so, and their style was unworthy of their vision. Rimbaud compares them amusingly to 'locomotives abandonnées, mais brûlantes, que prennent quelque temps les rails' (cf. Lautréamont's image of Musset, 'Nous sommes en présence du déraillement d'une locomotive surmenée'). The 'second Romantics' include such Parnassians as Gautier, Leconte de Lisle and Théodore de Banville, and these are 'très *voyants*'; but it is Baudelaire who receives the highest praise: 'le premier voyant, roi des poètes, *un vrai Dieu*'. Yet even he is criticised for expressing his visions of the new and the unknown in a literary, conventional style, and is condemned because of the 'meanness' of his form.

This massacre of the guilty, and of some innocents, is similar to the demolition by Rimbaud's contemporary Lautréamont of the 'Grandes-Têtes-Molles' of French literature. Both poets share the ideal of a society where 'official' poets and their subjective poetry would be replaced by an objective poetry, having a practical function which, in Lautréamont's words, would be 'faite par tous. Non par un'. But whereas he is almost clinical in his approach, and with one stroke of the scalpel disposes once and for all of the illustrious predecessors and contemporaries, Rimbaud seems to need them even while rejecting them – a psychological mechanism which was to operate throughout his life. He envelops them in the grand rhetorical sweep of his manifesto, measures himself against them, and uses them as a springboard for his own journey into the unknown.

The key to the *Lettre du voyant* is Rimbaud's discovery that 'Je est un autre' — a sentence used also in the Izambard letter. Out of its context, this could be interpreted as a philosophical statement about self-knowledge and the duality of the human personality; but the literary context in which it occurs shows that it refers to a special kind of 'inspired' poetry, and the way that poetry originates in the mind. Taking himself as an example, Rimbaud illustrates this by a series of concrete images:

> Si le cuivre s'éveille clairon, il n'y a rien de sa faute. Cela m'est évident: j'assiste à l'éclosion de ma pensée; je la regarde, je l'écoute: je lance un coup d'archet: la symphonie fait son remuement dans les profondeurs, ou vient d'un bond sur la scène.

It is ready-made poetry, Rimbaud implies, with a certain contempt. Just as brass is transformed into a bugle, or wood finds it has become a violin (the image in the Izambard letter), the 'I' becomes 'another', and poems erupt ready-formed into the mind. They are merely the result of a universal process, what Baudelaire had termed a 'mécanique céleste', to which Rimbaud himself, like the first and second Romantics, had submitted.

Rimbaud therefore decides that he must abandon such facile poetry in order to initiate a deliberate creative process whereby he will make himself a different kind of poet: a *voyant*. The first step is self-knowledge, and he declares: 'La première étude de l'homme qui veut être poète est sa propre connaissance, entière.' The stress is on the last word 'entière'. Rimbaud's intention is to go beyond all limits, whether those set by Greek wisdom or by Christian doctrine and morality. He will be the 'voleur de feu', 'le grand maudit', as well as 'le suprême Savant'. His view is exactly the opposite of that expressed by Pascal in the *Pensées*: 'Si l'homme s'étudiait le premier, il verrait combien il est incapable de passer outre.' 'Passer outre' is the very watchword of the *voyant*, and in the letter Rimbaud asserts:

> Le Poète se fait *voyant* par un long, immense et raisonné *dérèglement* de *tous les sens*. Toutes les formes d'amour, de souffrance, de folie; il cherche lui-même, il épuise en lui tous les poisons, pour n'en garder que les quintessences. Ineffable torture où il a besoin de toute la foi, de toute la force surhumaine, où il devient entre tous le grand malade, le grand criminel, le grand maudit, — et le suprême Savant! — Car il arrive à l'*inconnu*! Puisqu'il a cultivé son âme, déjà riche, plus qu'aucun! Il arrive à l'inconnu, et quand, affolé, il finirait par perdre l'intelligence de ses visions, il

les a vues! Qu'il crève dans son bondissement par les
choses inouies et innommables: viendront d'autres horribles travailleurs; ils commenceront par les horizons
où l'autre s'est affaissé!

In the first sentence of that amazing *art poétique*, the words 'se
fait' and 'raisonné' are as important as those Rimbaud himself
has underlined. Self-knowledge through conscious methodical
means — the active 'faire' and 'se faire' rather than the passive
'être' — is constantly stressed. The originality lies precisely in
the tremendous personal emphasis Rimbaud gives to his aim,
and, above all, in the unusual means he adopts to achieve it.
That poets are made as well as born is not an original idea.
Mallarmé, for example, who believed that a poet could completely change his manner of writing as he himself did, wrote in
a letter to Eugène Lefébure: 'Devant le papier, l'artiste *se fait.*'
Rimbaud is more ambitious, and it is not solely as a writer, in
isolated moments 'devant le papier', that he seeks to change
himself, but continuously and totally, as both writer and man,
through the actual process of living. In pursuit of this, he experi-
mented with every possible kind of indulgence and privation,
excessive work and extreme fatigue, the taking of drugs, anything calculated to produce an abnormal state of mind; and to
this monstrous 'cultivation' of his genius he dedicated the rest
of his career.
About the positive aspects of his creed, Rimbaud is, of neces-
sity, rather vague, and in particular about the manner of expressing the new visions and the unknown. Having escaped from
the confining shell of a traditional style, the poet must find
another language, but his cry 'Trouver une langue' is less an
order or an exhortation than the statement of a problem and a
challenge. The poet should be free in his quest, and faithful to
his vision, for it is the nature of the vision, of what is seen or
only partly seen, that determines the form, or the formlessness,
of the expression: 'si ce qu'il rapporte de *là-bas* a forme, il donne
forme; si c'est informe, il donne de l'informe'. Expression and
vision are intimately related, as are the ideas about finding a
language and being responsible for humanity and changing life.
Rimbaud is concerned with the second as much as with the first
of these aims, and he extends his ideas beyond poetry to include

a universal language, capable of expressing all sensations and all thoughts. He envisages a society in which poetry would be a consciously achieved *œuvre*, at once objective and subjective: more dynamic than Greek poetry and more visionary than Romantic poetry, with the power to shape as well as to foresee the future. The poet himself, his duties extending to all mankind, would be not only a creator and a visionary, but also a *'multiplicateur de progrès'*.

In the conclusion to the letter, Rimbaud repeats the main theme: 'Ainsi je travaille à me rendre *voyant.*' That statement on 15 May 1871 is at the centre of his poetic creed, and it gives bearings for his future development. The *Lettre du voyant* is essential to an understanding of all the poems written after that date, and in particular of the *Illuminations* and *Une Saison en enfer.* Using not only words but *himself* in the search for visions, Rimbaud stakes all on his programme of self-inflicted suffering as he advances towards an unpredictable future.

4

FROM POET TO *VOYANT*

Another letter, dated 10 June 1871, which Rimbaud sent to Demeny, throws further light on this critical stage in his development. 'Brûlez, *je le veux*', he wrote, 'et je crois que vous respecterez ma volonté comme celle d'un mort, brûlez *tous les vers que je fus assez sot* pour vous donner lors de mon séjour à Douai.' Fortunately, Demeny did not burn these poems, which include one or two minor masterpieces, among them 'Ma Bohème', 'Les Effarés' and 'À la musique'. Rimbaud's request, or 'prière' as he calls it in the letter, was typical, for throughout his career development and renunciation go hand in hand. It was also sincere, revealing a profound dissatisfaction with poems he had written only a few months previously. He was, however, clearly pleased with his subsequent progress, for he enclosed three examples of his recent poetry — 'Les Pauvres à l'église', 'Le Cœur du pitre'[4] and 'Les Poètes de sept ans' — with the statement: 'Voilà ce que je fais.'

Of these, 'Les Pauvres à l'église' is the least original; but it may have been added because it is Rimbaud's fiercest and most comprehensive attack on the Church, God and a Christianity which enslaves people with its false consolations and reduces them to the state of docile, stupid animals. 'Le Cœur du pitre', on the other hand, is a striking example of his skill in introducing an unusually robust, 'modern' vocabulary into a traditional stanza form and giving it fresh life. Even if the poem does not record, as some critics maintain it does, a humiliating experience or 'terrible initiation' which Rimbaud underwent in Paris in May 1871 at the time of the Commune (there is no proof that he was actually there during the uprising), the intensity of the feeling may derive in part from his disillusionment at the failure of the people's revolt. In 'Les Mains de Jeanne-Marie' he had exalted with magnificent rhetoric the heroic hands of a *communarde*; but in 'Le Cœur volé' the cry is of personal loss and disarray, all the more poignant because it is expressed in the ingenious rhymes and frivolous metres of a triolet, the only one Rimbaud ever wrote.

LE CŒUR VOLÉ

Mon triste cœur bave à la poupe,
Mon cœur couvert de caporal:
Ils y lancent des jets de soupe,
Mon triste cœur bave à la poupe:
Sous les quolibets de la troupe
Qui pousse un rire général,
Mon triste cœur bave à la poupe,
Mon cœur couvert de caporal!

Ithyphalliques et pioupiesques
Leurs quolibets l'ont dépravé!
Au gouvernail on voit des fresques
Ithyphalliques et pioupiesques.
Ô flots abracadabrantesques,
Prenez mon cœur, qu'il soit lavé!
Ithyphalliques et pioupiesques
Leurs quolibets l'ont dépravé!

Quand ils auront tari leurs chiques,
Comment agir, ô cœur volé?
Ce seront des hoquets bachiques
Quand ils auront tari leurs chiques:
J'aurai des sursauts stomachiques,
Moi, si mon cœur est ravalé:
Quand ils auront tari leurs chiques
Comment agir, ô cœur volé?

'Les Poètes de sept ans', Rimbaud's only autobiographical poem, is dated '26 mai 1871', though Izambard always maintained, against the opinion of critics, that it was written seven or eight months earlier. The fact that Rimbaud did copy it out and send it to Demeny in June shows that he was pleased with it, and that he felt it represented, like the other two poems, a further stage in his development. As Ernest Delahaye wrote in *Rimbaud, l'artiste et l'être moral*, it is a poem which, despite 'plusieurs lignes "objectionables"', must be read in order to initiate oneself into Rimbaud's work.[2] In this realistic poem, Rimbaud looks back ten years to the time when he was seven years old, and speaks for himself and for other children, the 'poètes de sept ans' who, like him, had been frustrated in their youth. The same critical eye with which he had surveyed the inhabitants of his native town in the bourgeois scene of 'À la musique' is now directed onto himself and his past life; but with an ironic sympathy for the working-class children who were his only friends, and for himself in his rebellion against his mother:

À M. P. Demeny

LES POÈTES DE SEPT ANS

Et la Mère, fermant le livre du devoir,
S'en allait satisfaite et très fière, sans voir,
Dans les yeux bleus et sous le front plein d'éminences,
L'âme de son enfant livrée aux répugnances.

Tout le jour il suait d'obéissance; très
Intelligent; pourtant des tics noirs, quelques traits
Semblaient prouver en lui d'âcres hypocrisies.
Dans l'ombre des couloirs aux tentures moisies,
En passant il tirait la langue, les deux poings
À l'aine, et dans ses yeux fermés voyait des points.
Une porte s'ouvrait sur le soir : à la lampe
On le voyait, là-haut, qui râlait sur la rampe,
Sous un golfe de jour pendant du toit. L'été
Surtout, vaincu, stupide, il était entêté
À se renfermer dans la fraîcheur des latrines :
Il pensait là, tranquille et livrant ses narines.

Quand, lavé des odeurs du jour le jardinet
Derrière la maison, en hiver, s'illunait,
Gisant au pied d'un mur, enterré dans la marne
Et pour des visions écrasant son œil darne,
Il écoutait grouiller les galeux espaliers.
Pitié! Ces enfants seuls étaient ses familiers
Qui, chétifs, fronts nus, œil déteignant sur la joue,
Cachant de maigres doigts jaunes et noirs de boue
Sous des habits puant la foire et tout vieillots,
Conversaient avec la douceur des idiots!
Et si, l'ayant surpris à des pitiés immondes,

Sa mère s'effrayait; les tendresses, profondes,
De l'enfant se jetaient sur cet étonnement.
C'était bon. Elle avait le bleu regard, —qui ment!

À sept ans, il faisait des romans, sur la vie
Du grand désert où luit la Liberté ravie,
Forêts, soleils, rives, savanes! —Il s'aidait
De journaux illustrés où, rouge, il regardait
Des Espagnoles rire et des Italiennes.

Quand venait, l'œil brun, folle, en robes d'indiennes,
—Huit ans, —la fille des ouvriers d'à côté,
La petite brutale, et qu'elle avait sauté,
Dans un coin, sur son dos, en secouant ses tresses,
Et qu'il était sous elle, il lui mordait les fesses,
Car elle ne portait jamais de pantalons;
—Et, par elle meurtri des poings et des talons,
Remportait les saveurs de sa peau dans sa chambre.

Il craignait les blafards dimanches de décembre,
Où, pommadé, sur un guéridon d'acajou,
Il lisait une Bible à la tranche vert-chou;
Des rêves l'oppressaient chaque nuit dans l'alcôve.
Il n'aimait pas Dieu; mais les hommes, qu'au soir fauve,
Noirs, en blouse, il voyait rentrer dans le faubourg
Où les crieurs, en trois roulements de tambour,
Font autour des édits rire et gronder les foules.
— Il rêvait la prairie amoureuse, où des houles
Lumineuses, parfums sains, pubescences d'or,
Font leur remuement calme et prennent leur essor!

Et comme il savourait surtout les sombres choses,
Quand, dans la chambre nue aux persiennes closes,
Haute et bleue, âcrement prise d'humidité,
Il lisait son roman sans cesse médité,
Plein de lourds ciels ocreux et de forêts noyées,
De fleurs de chair aux bois sidérals déployées,
Vertige, écroulements, déroutes et pitié!
— Tandis que se faisait la rumeur du quartier,
En bas, —seul, et couché sur des pièces de toile
Écrue, et pressentant violemment la voile!

The 'Et' which starts the poem and is used five more times

at the beginning of lines, gives it an air of spontaneity, as if it were a page torn from a diary; but it also suggests that it may have been built up line by line, or section by section, rather than conceived as a whole. Structurally, 'Les Poètes de sept ans' is less finished than an 'exercise' like 'Le Buffet', and less coherent than a major poem like 'Mémoire', where the experience has been not only lived but reflected upon, modified and fused into a synthesis. Artistry is apparent, however, in the references to the poet-narrator as 'il', 'le' and 'lui', and in the way distance and an appearance of objectivity are given by the use of the past tense throughout, while at the same time the characters and the successive scenes are brought vividly before us. The urban background is evoked by a few concrete notations, 'faubourg', 'ouvriers', 'les hommes noirs ... en blouse', 'les crieurs', 'les foules', and more delicately by a phrase that echoes Verlaine, 'la rumeur du quartier'; and aspects of nature, 'la prairie amoureuse', flowers, skies and forests are not described, as they had been in previous poems, but are presented as part of the poet's dreams and visions.

The brief dramatic evocation of the smouldering revolt of the intelligent child against the uncomprehending mother, 'aussi inflexible que soixante-treize administrations à casquettes de plomb' as Rimbaud described her in a letter,[3] is followed by a full-length picture of himself in the confined setting of his Charleville home. The personal nature and the authenticity of this sharply particularised picture are strikingly apparent. The child-poet is presented physically, from the outside, with his sinister 'tics' and defiant gestures, and in unexpected places and from curiously angled viewpoints. He is also depicted in a more intimate way, with his sensuous savouring of every kind of experience; his dreams of escape and freedom; his hatred of God and his love of mankind; the awakening of his sexual desires and of his imagination; and the beginning of his search for visions: 'Et pour des visions écrasant son œil darne'. This gesture, like that in line 10 ('... et dans ses yeux fermés voyait des points'), belongs to childhood, for every child has rubbed or screwed up his eyes in this way. For Rimbaud, however, the action expresses a desire to escape from reality, to see differently and to force visions from within himself. This not only reinforces the importance of the seeing eyes of the child, it indicates

the relationship between his world and the world of the *voyant*.
'Les Poètes de sept ans', as well as being an important critical
survey of Rimbaud's own childhood, is the culmination of a
series of portraits of children, of adults, of the poet himself, that
are unique in French literature.

Rimbaud's confidence in the new poetic theory towards
which he was striving is illustrated in a poem which he sent to
Théodore de Banville on 15 August 1871. This was 'Ce qu' on dit
au poète à propos de fleurs', consisting of forty stanzas, each
of four octosyllabic lines, signed 'Alcide Bava' and dated 14 July
1871. The pseudonym Alcide Bava (Alcide, a name for Hercules,
and Bava from *baver*, 'to slobber') and the date (the anniversary
of the fall of the Bastille) reveal Rimbaud's scorn, and his aware-
ness of the Herculean task of storming, as Hugo did before him,
poetic conventions and 'la bastille des rimes'; and a comparison
between this poem and the three — 'Sensation', 'Ophélie' and
'Soleil et chair' — which he had sent to Banville on 24 May 1870
certainly shows the astonishing progress he had made in little
more than a year. In that time he had outgrown the influence
of the Parnassian school and could now surpass the master in
originality of vocabulary, versification, rhymes and images. The
poem is a pastiche, in places a parody of Banville; but it is also
a semi-serious application of Rimbaud's new theories, and an
address to poets in general. After ridiculing, with an exuberance
of mordant wit and fancy, the flowers of Parnassian poetry —
lilies, lilacs, violets and roses (some of which he himself had
once used) — he dismisses them as a 'Tas d'œufs frits dans de
vieux chapeaux'. He then proceeds to make positive recommen-
dations similar to those he had made in the *Lettre du voyant*: art
should have a useful, social function; the poet must know himself and his subject; in a world where the 'songs of iron' of tele-
graph wires have replaced the lyre, he must find fresh sources
of inspiration in commerce, science, industry and technology;
he must look towards the future and be in the vanguard of
progress. Rimbaud provocatively suggests subjects such as
rubber, cotton and tobacco; syrups, gums, resins and guano;
sago, starch and sugar. He ends with the command:

> Surtout, rime une version
> Sur le mal des pommes de terre!

This final shaft directed against the faded flora of the Parnassians may also be a derisive allusion to Musset's and the first Romantics' theme of *le mal du siècle*, and to Baudelaire's *Fleurs du mal*. But while demonstrating, with an appropriate choice of technical terms and original images, the possibilities of this more scientific approach to the universe, Rimbaud himself never seriously considers treating the inexhaustible themes made available by the industrial age. The mocking tone of this satirical poem suggests that, although demanding complete artistic freedom in the search for subjects, he is holding himself in reserve for something more important than the merely new, or the reconciliation of beauty and utility, of art and science. His affair is with *l'inconnu* – the unknown, and a language in which it could be expressed.

—In 'Voyelles' Rimbaud addresses language; this sonnet, along with 'L'étoile a pleuré rose ...', and 'Le Bateau ivre', is among the first experiments in composing the new visionary poetry adumbrated in the *Lettre du voyant*. It is almost certainly the last of the fourteen sonnets written in the period 1870–1, and it is perhaps the most famous of all Rimbaud's poems. Verlaine was the first to publish it in 1883 in the review *Lutèce*; and the following year, in his volume *Les Poètes maudits*, he gave it pride of place among the Rimbaud poems, commenting on the versification and the vocabulary and, despite obscurities in the meaning, on the strength and clarity of the language. When he published it again five years later in *Les Hommes d'aujourd'hui*, with Luque's amusing caricature of Rimbaud painting the vowels, he referred to some of the 'superbes vers' and to 'l'intense beauté' of the sonnet; and warned readers against treating this 'chef-d'œuvre' as a scientific document or the statement of a theory. The advice was necessary, for already some of the Symbolists were attempting to extract from it elaborate theories of synaesthesia and 'coloured hearing', which have since been dismissed as subjective and unscientific. These were followed, early in the twentieth century, by a more reasonable approach based on the belief that 'Voyelles' had been inspired by a child's printed alphabet, with coloured letters and pictures; but those who explored this hypothesis treated the text as if it were a crossword puzzle, and stressed possible solutions (such as, A-Abeille; E—Eau; I—Indien or Iroquois; U—Univers; O—Orgue and Œil) rather than the creative process. More recently, 'Voyelles' has been subjected to a number of exhaustive inter- pretations — psychological, occult, alchemical, cabalistic, mys- tical, pseudo-scientific and erotic.[4] Whatever their merits, these interpretations do at least show that this sonnet continues to exert an enigmatic attraction; but, as is the risk with ingenious theories, attention has been diverted from the actual text, and so from the fact that 'Voyelles' is, as Verlaine emphasised, first and last a poem. Verlaine may have overpraised it; but undoub- tedly he indicated the right approach.[5]

VOYELLES

A noir, E blanc, I rouge, U vert, O bleu: voyelles,
Je dirai quelque jour vos naissances latentes:
A, noir corset velu des mouches éclatantes
Qui bombinent autour des puanteurs cruelles,

Golfes d'ombre; E, candeurs des vapeurs et des tentes,
Lances des glaciers fiers, rois blancs, frissons d'ombelles;
I, pourpres, sang craché, rire des lèvres belles
Dans la colère ou les ivresses pénitentes;

U, cycles, vibrements divins des mers virides,
Paix des pâtis semés d'animaux, paix des rides
Que l'alchimie imprime aux grands fronts studieux;

O, suprême Clairon plein des strideurs étranges,
Silences traversés des Mondes et des Anges:
— O l'Oméga, rayon violet de Ses Yeux!

The vowels are seen as an essential part of the poet's raw material, language; and Rimbaud addresses them in a sentence which indicates the tentative, experimental nature of the son- net: 'Je dirai quelque jour vos naissances latentes.' The 'attack', 'A noir ...' is as characteristically abrupt as in 'Les Effarés', 'Noirs dans la neige et dans la brume'; but instead of narrating, describing or expressing personal feelings or ideas, Rimbaud is in a state of receptivity as he seeks to make language itself produce images and visions. It is like a play in which he allots a different colour to each vowel, then watches them act their roles, and sees what they create. The first line 'A noir, E blanc, I rouge, U vert, O bleu: voyelles' may suggest the voice of a child learning an alphabet; but it is also the voice of the *voyant* using words in a new creative way. He is, as Auden put it (echoing Verlaine), the adolescent strangling an old rhetoric; but, more than that, he is illustrating his new poetic theory and, in particular, his statement:

Cette langue sera de l'âme pour l'âme résumant tout, parfums, sons, couleurs, de la pensée accrochant la pensée et tirant.

Before puzzling over details, or asking what they mean, it is important to perceive the overall pattern, within which all details have a function and a meaning. Even at a first reading we are aware of a rhythmic movement and a progression from one vowel and one colour to a series of related and contrasted images, leading to a cosmic vision. We are also conscious of another more general and deeper progression, an upward surge from darkness to light, from the material to the spiritual, as we move from the contrasts and oppositions in the octave to the more flowing sestet which, particularly in the last stanza, is pervaded by a sense of space and light, and the mystery of the unknown. To end with 'Ses Yeux' seems entirely appropriate in a poem about vision.

One of the reasons for Rimbaud's choice of these five colours may have been that they represent the way he himself saw or 'coloured' the external world; and indeed, according to word counts, they are the five colours that occur most frequently in the verse poems. There is also the possibility that he chose red and blue because they are at opposite ends of the spectrum, and green because it is between the two. But a more likely and important source may have been Baudelaire's article 'De la couleur' about colours in a landscape, where everything is in 'perpetual vibration'. In this, black is the 'zéro solitaire et insignifiant' which pleads for the help of blue or red; the vitality of red sings to the glory of its complementary colour green, nature's fundamental colour; while blue, as in 'Voyelles', is the sky which, like 'la vapeur de la saison', softens all contours. Rimbaud's order of the colours — two contrasts, black and white, followed by two complementaries, red and green, then a primary, blue, rich in symbolic associations — may have been determined mainly by aesthetic considerations. For similar reasons, he modified the normal order of the vowels, putting

'O' after 'U' probably to avoid the hiatus 'O bleu, U vert'; and in
order to end with 'O', whose shape represents the trumpet of the
Last Judgement, and with Omega, the last letter of the Greek
alphabet, which recalls the biblical 'I am Alpha and Omega,
the beginning and the end, the first and the last' (Revelation
22 : 13, also Revelation 1 : 8 and 21 : 6).

The simplest and perhaps most profitable way to read 'Voyelles' is to examine how each vowel suggests things of its particular colour. Those evoked by 'A noir' appeal to four of the
senses: sight ('noir'), sound ('bombinent', an onomatopoeic
verb invented by Rimbaud from the Latin *bombinare*, 'to hum'
or 'to buzz'), touch ('velu') and smell ('puanteurs'). Although
there is nothing exceptional about these sensuous images,
Rimbaud may have had in mind his aim of making poetry
'accessible, un jour ou l'autre, à tous les sens'. But this experiment is not pursued in the rest of the sonnet. From 'E blanc'
springs a sequence of visual images suggesting (in addition to
whiteness) purity, freshness, vitality, pride, power − all in as
marked contrast to the 'golfes d'ombre' of 'A noir' as the sound
of the quivering of the umbelliferous flowers is to the buzzing
of the flies. 'I', in lines at once balanced and opposed, evokes
red objects, blood and lips, which in turn express two mental
states, anger and intoxication. With one word, 'cycles', the 'U'
widens the perspective to embrace the world of nature; and
green ('mers virides') is linked to cyclical movements, tides,
seasons, growth and so on, and, through the green of the
pastures ('pâtis semés d'animaux'), to calm and stillness.
Finally, through a likeness between the furrowed brow of the
alchemist and the waves of the sea, man and his wisdom are
included in this spacious vision. The use and the position of the
superlative 'suprême', and the introduction of six capital letters,
give the last vowel 'O' and the conclusion a special significance.
'Ses Yeux', which has puzzled all commentators, may be the
eyes of God, or the eyes of the sky (cf. 'les yeux de l'Azur' in
Verlaine's 'Art poétique'), under whose violet canopy the opposites, 'strideurs' and 'silences', exist in harmony. More probably, they are the eyes of the poet, the 'suprême Savant' and
voyant. It is characteristic of Rimbaud to conclude on a challenging enigmatic note, giving at the end of the poem its origin and
source, the poet's eyes and his vision of the world. In doing so,

he has also conformed to the usual pattern of the sonnet, where the last line should contain an ingenious device, or, as Banville said, 'la pensée du Sonnet tout entière'.

As regards technique this, like his other sonnets, is slightly irregular, yet without showing any striking originality of form. In fact, it bears marks of its period, and certain words — the Latinism 'virides', and abstract nouns used in the plural, such as 'puanteurs', 'candeurs', 'pourpres' —belong to a decadent symbolist vocabulary. Yet, in this sonnet where there are few verbs, and isolated words and images are more important than the logic of a sentence, there is something fundamentally new. Rimbaud is attempting to communicate in a less rational and more direct way, using language itself as his theme, and allowing it, in Mallarmé's words, to 'take the initiative'. 'Voyelles' is an important linguistic experiment, which has inspired painters like Delaunay, sculptors such as Tilson, and today the Spatialist poets, among them Pierre Garnier. Yet while it demonstrates Rimbaud's mastery of the elements of language, it is fragmentary. The colours of his universe are not related to any central idea and they do not 'reply' to each other as do the colours, scents and sounds in Baudelaire's sonnet 'Correspondances', with which 'Voyelles' is often compared. Separate, and stretched out in lines, they fail to coalesce into the clear vision of the *voyant*; a 'failure' which the poet himself recognised later in his cynical comment in *Une Saison en enfer*:

J'inventai la couleur des voyelles! — *A* noir, *E* blanc, *I* rouge, *O* bleu, *U* vert. — Je réglai la forme et le mouvement de chaque consonne, et, avec des rhythmes instinctifs, je me flattai d'inventer un verbe poétique accessible, un jour ou l'autre, à tous les sens.

The experiment in 'Voyelles' yielded a by-product, a quatrain perfect in form and content, one of Rimbaud's rare calm poems. Colours, instead of existing in isolation or standing out too vividly as in 'Voyelles', are related to one object, subordinated to a single theme, and blended into the texture of the poem:

L'étoile a pleuré rose au cœur œ tes oreilles,
L'infini roulé blanc de ta nuque à tes reins
La mer a perlé rousse à tes mammes vermeilles
Et l'Homme saigné noir à ton flanc souverain.

As well as colour, there is nuance; and the contrast between white and black, essential to the theme, is all the more effective because of the 'rose' and the 'rousse'. Instead of rhetorical flourishes and exclamations, there are devices such as the closely related expressions 'a pleuré rose' and 'a perlé rousse', which are both logical and evocative; and in place of the obtrusive alliteration in 'Voyelles', the alliterative effects are discreet and functional (to take one example, compare the recurrence of 'v' in 1.9 of 'Voyelles' with that of 'r' in ll. 1 and 4 of the quatrain). Similarly, the single capital letter 'H' of 'l'Homme' is neither decorative nor emblematic, as are the capitals in the last stanza of 'Voyelles': it conveys man's arrogant irresponsibility for what he has made of woman and the world of nature. This 'song of experience', comparable to poems of Blake such as 'The Clod and the Pebble', 'The Sick Rose', 'The Lily', has the simplicity and the inevitability of great poetry; and its theme is even more relevant today than when the poem was written.

The *voyant* theory is applied in a more extended form in 'Le Bateau ivre'. This is one of the best-known of Rimbaud's poems, and one that has elicited innumerable commentaries, ecstatic appreciations, and recently a few critical broadsides. It was written in 1871 specially for 'les gens de Paris', after Rimbaud had accepted Verlaine's urgent invitation to visit the literary circles in the capital: 'Venez, chère grande âme, on vous appelle, on vous attend!' On the eve of his departure he read the poem to Ernest Delahaye, his friend and confidant for more than ten years, and his reported reply to his friend's enthusiastic comments, 'Ah! oui on n'a rien écrit de semblable, je le sais bien', suggests that he realised fully the originality of his work. This originality, however, does not lie in the form; indeed, in this respect the poem belongs to what Verlaine called 'la grande Rhétorique'. The rules and conventions are observed in the twenty-five quatrains with their alternate feminine and masculine rhymes, and in the alexandrines with, apart from a few exceptions, four main stresses, and the caesura after the sixth syllable. Moreover, there had been predecessors. Some critics, reluctant to acknowledge Rimbaud's originality, indeed unable to believe in it, have endeavoured to discover 'sources' in the works of Chateaubriand, Lamartine, Hugo, Edgar Allan Poe, Gautier, Leconte de Lisle, Jules Verne, Verlaine, and in that inexhaustible treasure trove, the twenty-one volumes of the illustrated periodical, *Le Magasin pittoresque*, which Rimbaud is supposed to have read at Douai. Also cited are the works of Captain Cook, and even a banal poem about a boat, 'Le Vieux Solitaire' by Léon Dierx, whose name, it is true, appears in the *Lettre du voyant* (along with Sully Prudhomme and Coppée) as one of the 'talents'. But Rimbaud's 'difference' and his originality are more apparent if one compares him with 'le premier voyant', Baudelaire, and examines the relationship, first observed by Gustave Kahn as early as 1902 in *Symbolistes et décadents*, between 'Le Voyage' and 'Le Bateau ivre'.[6]

In 'Le Voyage', Baudelaire looks back on a lived experience, a journey through life to a known end: boredom, pessimism, and the bitter conviction that only sin and death are immortal. Rimbaud, on the other hand, writes from within the immediate experience of an imagined world, as it reveals the exciting possibilities of unexplored horizons. He had never seen the sea, and the originality of his 'Poème de la Mer' lies in the visions he sees with the eye of the mind. He is completely identified with his theme. He and the boat are one, and its experiences are his — the break with civilisation; the quest for the unknown; the exhilarating taste of freedom; the innumerable visions, some dangerous and awe-inspiring, others beautiful and reassuring; the conflicting sensations and emotions as extreme as the climate of the 'poles' and the 'zones' of the poem; the longing for the 'future Vigueur', followed by a desire for death or nothingness; the nostalgia for Europe and childhood; and finally frustration, lassitude and exhaustion. In 'Le Bateau ivre' Rimbaud acts upon and translates into poetry what Baudelaire had only proclaimed as an intention or a desperate wish, the search for 'l'Inconnu' and 'du *nouveau*'. His poem is a triumphant reply to the challenge on which 'Le Voyage' ends:

> Verse-nous ton poison pour qu'il nous réconforte!
> Nous voulons, tant ce feu nous brûle le cerveau,
> Plonger au fond du gouffre, Enfer ou Ciel, qu'importe?
> Au fond de l'Inconnu pour trouver du *nouveau*!

The duality of hell and heaven, guilt and innocence, does not yet exist for Rimbaud, and his attitude is the amoral one of the child. He is, as he says in the poem, 'plus sourd que les cerveaux

d'enfants', and he rejects all moral and social restraints in his
search for 'l'Inconnu'. He does not merely talk about plunging to
the depths of the abyss; that experience is his among many
wonderful and terrifying visions:

> Je sais les cieux crevant en éclairs, et les trombes
> Et les ressacs et les courants: je sais le soir,
> L'Aube exaltée ainsi qu'un peuple de colombes,
> Et j'ai vu quelquefois ce que l'homme a cru voir!
>
> J'ai vu le soleil bas, taché d'horreurs mystiques,
> Illuminant de longs figements violets,
> Pareils à des acteurs de drames très-antiques
> Les flots roulant au loin leurs frissons de volets!
>
> J'ai rêvé la nuit verte aux neiges éblouies,
> Baiser montant aux yeux des mers avec lenteurs,
> La circulation des sèves inouïes,
> Et l'éveil jaune et bleu des phosphores chanteurs!
>
> J'ai suivi, des mois pleins, pareille aux vacheries
> Hystériques, la houle à l'assaut des récifs,
> Sans songer que les pieds lumineux des Maries
> Pussent forcer le mufle aux Océans poussifs!
>
> J'ai heurté, savez-vous, d'incroyables Florides
> Mêlant aux fleurs des yeux de panthères à peaux
> D'hommes! Des arcs-en-ciel tendus comme des brides
> Sous l'horizon des mers, à de glauques troupeaux!
>
> J'ai vu fermenter les marais énormes, nasses
> Où pourrit dans les joncs tout un Léviathan!
> Des écroulements d'eaux au milieu des bonaces,
> Et les lointains vers les gouffres cataractant!

'Je sais', 'J'ai vu' and numerous other verbs at the beginning
of stanzas, and also within them, are like a reply to the question
Baudelaire asked the travellers in 'Le Voyage': 'Dites, qu'avez-
vous vu?' But whereas they respond with tourist-like recollec-
tions and banal memories, Rimbaud as the 'bateau ivre' is
immersed in a series of kaleidoscopic visions, and his statements
have the immediacy of direct experience. The images in
Baudelaire's poem are used to illustrate the pessimistic theme
of ennui and sin, 'Le spectacle ennuyeux de l'immortel péché',

and to show that man's restless journeyings only reveal the smallness of his universe. In 'Le Bateau ivre', there is no pessimism and no moral intention — to see is an end in itself, and the images are self-sufficient. They have no theme and no message other than to say, 'we are new' with a force that is dynamic and explosive. Sartre described 'Le Bateau ivre' as an 'éclatement glorieux de l'étendue', and said of the image of the dawn, 'Voir en l'aube un "peuple de colombes" c'est faire sauter le matin comme une poudrière', while other critics have described this powerful force as 'dionysiac', 'conquering', 'dynamic', 'centrifugal'. Its only unity is not, however, as Sartre implied, 'une unité explosive'. It is one of opposites and extremes which, from the first to the last stanza, are linked by a wave-like movement, rising and falling, and finally, its force spent, returning to the world of childhood:

Moi qui tremblais, sentant geindre à cinquante lieues
Le rut des Béhémots et les Maelstroms épais,
Fileur éternel des immobilités bleues,
Je regrette l'Europe aux anciens parapets!

J'ai vu des archipels sidéraux! et des îles
Dont les cieux délirants sont ouverts au vogueur:
— Est-ce en ces nuits sans fond que tu dors et t'exiles,
Million d'oiseaux d'or, ô future Vigueur? —

Mais, vrai, j'ai trop pleuré! Les Aubes sont navrantes.
Toute lune est atroce et tout soleil amer:
L'âcre amour m'a gonflé de torpeurs enivrantes.
Ô que ma quille éclate! Ô que j'aille à la mer!

Si je désire une eau d'Europe, c'est la flache
Noire et froide où vers le crépuscule embaumé
Un enfant accroupi plein de tristesses, lâche
Un bateau frêle comme un papillon de mai.

Je ne puis plus, baigné de vos langueurs, ô lames,
Enlever leur sillage aux porteurs de cotons,
Ni traverser l'orgueil des drapeaux et des flammes,
Ni nager sous les yeux horribles des pontons.

It may be a coincidence, and if so a strange one, that this long visionary poem should end, like the sonnet 'Voyelles', with a reference in the last line to eyes. But here the 'eyes' are the

sinister lights of the prison ships, which represent all that op-
poses the poet's desire for freedom. They are eyes which threaten
to extinguish his vision: they symbolise his defeat and the end
of his adventure. The last two stanzas are, however, ambiguous,
as Rimbaud thinks again of 'l'Europe aux anciens parapets',
and of childhood, from both of which he had cut himself
adrift with brutal impetuosity at the beginning of the poem. The
'si' in 'si je désire' can be read as an 'if of supposition, 'if I want',
or, more emphatically (as Samuel Beckett translated it), 'I want
none of Europe's waters unless it be the cold black puddle . . .';[8]
or it can be the opposite, a rhetorical way of stating a fact, 'I
do want.' Everything in the penultimate stanza is in ironic
contrast to the rest of the poem: the puddle with the ocean; the
cold blackness with the constantly changing colours and scenes;
the fragile boat — a child's plaything — with the drunken boat of
poetry. There is certainly disenchantment and frustration
because the new source of inspiration, the 'future Vigueur' which
he had imagined as a 'million d'oiseaux d'or', has escaped him.
The poem ends on a tone of exasperated weariness, with a
series of negations. Yet although the vision is darkened and
diminished, the twilight is fragrant, and the child, full of sadness,
still has enough faith to launch his boat, frail but beautiful as
a May butterfly. The whole stanza is, by its evocative power,
pure lyricism and imagery, a poetic triumph over failure and
defeat.

   In whatever way the concluding stanzas are interpreted,
the tone of the statement 'Je ne puis plus, baigné de vos langueurs, ô lames' is very different from that in the sixth stanza
'Et dès lors, je me suis baigné dans le Poème de la Mer'. Rimbaud
has been changed. He is no longer able or willing to follow in the
wake of the merchant ships or to brave the prison hulks, symbols
of the traffickings and tyrannies of society. The 'bateau frêle
comme un papillon de mai' marks the end of one experience
and the beginning of another. It is the symbol of a quite different poetic adventure, which reaches its climax in the *Illuminations*.

At this point, it may be useful to look back briefly at the various
stages of Rimbaud's progress, which can be traced not only in
the themes but also in the changing versification, vocabulary

and style. In acquiring a technique, his attitude was, as in other matters, one of aggression; more than most writers, he seems to have needed opponents rather than models in order to find himself. This he did quickly, with bravado and panache, and it was while disposing of Romantic poets such as Lamartine, Musset and Hugo (the Hugo of *Les Châtiments*) and numerous Parnassians — Banville, Leconte de Lisle, Coppée, Glatigny, Léon Dierx and Albert Mérat — that he discovered his own authentic tone of voice.

Aspects of this evolution, or what might better be called a subversive apprenticeship, have been examined in some detail (though from the outside) by François Ruchon in his book *Jean-Arthur Rimbaud, sa vie, son œuvre, son influence* (1929).[9] Ruchon shows how Rimbaud, after using the classical alexandrine and experimenting with its Romantic version, the trimeter, moved on to become, through his adoption of freer and more flexible metres and verse forms, the forerunner of the Symbolists. He also gives lists of lexical peculiarities and innovations (without however discussing them in their contexts): nouns formed from rare or archaic words ('bleuison', 'ostiaire', 'pandiculations', 'strideurs', etc.); abstract nouns used in the plural, which was later to become a Symbolist tic of style ('bêtises', 'blondeurs', 'immobilités', 'silences', etc.); neologisms ('bombiner', 'percaliser', 'robinsonner', 'hargnosités', etc.); dialectical terms used in the Ardennes ('darne' — 'giddy'; 'éclanches' — 'shoulders'; 'fesses' — 'branches'; 'fouffes' — 'rags'; etc.); scientific and medical terms, some of which Rimbaud was the first to use in a poetic vocabulary ('sodium', 'phosphore', 'hydrogène', 'hydrolat', 'astéroïdes', 'dioptique', 'pectoraire', 'cataplasme', 'clystère', 'embryon', 'fémur', 'ulcère', 'omoplate', 'ovaire', 'amygdales', 'hypogastre', 'sinciput', 'ossature', 'céphalagies', etc.). Some of these scientific and medical terms are deployed with polemical effectiveness in 'Ce qu'on dit au poète à propos de fleurs', but their use is diverse and widespread in all the verse poems.

Anatomical terms, together with a profusion of non-scientific words frequently and repetitiously used for parts of the body ('ventre', for example, occurs fifteen times in the *Poésies*), are of exceptional significance. They are used not solely for their novelty nor, as Ruchon suggests, merely to surprise and shock;

they reflect a fascinated and obsessive interest, at all levels, in the human body. This obsession has many ramifications and some extreme forms, ranging from the coprophilic interest of the child in 'Les Poètes de sept ans' seeking refuge and 'livrant ses narines' in the coolness of the lavatory, and the contorted 'accroupissements' of brother Milotus, to the poet, 'accroupi, plein de tristesses', who launches his frail boat at the end of 'Le Bateau ivre'. The obsession manifests itself, or rather is consciously used, in a great variety of ways: in tactical assaults on established values and responses ('Vénus anadyomène'), to express tenderness and compassion ('Le Dormeur du val'), for caricatural description ('Les Assis'), with sadistic venom ('Mes petites amoureuses'), to extol a noble revolutionary force ('Les Mains de Jeanne-Marie'), to produce original images and also (as in 'Les Chercheuses de poux') sharp, witty contrasts and delicate effects of sound echoing sense.

Many more examples could be given, but interesting and revealing as they are when studied in their contexts, their full significance is apparent only when they are seen in the broader perspective of Rimbaud's genius in animating and dramatising scenes, and indeed entire poems. In nearly all his pre-*voyant* poetry he is concerned to make us aware of the physically active presence of himself, the producer and stage-manager, and of all the characters (projections of himself), with their postures, gestures and speech. In this process, the words themselves seem physically alive and more than usually 'real'. Obvious examples of this dramatisation are 'Le Forgeron', 'À la musique', 'Les Effarés', 'La Maline', 'Oraison du soir', 'Accroupissements', 'Les Poètes de sept ans', 'Les Premières communions', and in these Rimbaud's artifices —anatomical and other more vigorous expressions, together with repetition, alliteration, enjambement, *rimes riches* and adjectives of colour (alone or in twos) — are mobilised to produce the maximum effect.

This interest in the human body and its use as a potent dramatising force, which is a major and constant factor in the *Poésies*, becomes progressively less physical and more aesthetically refined as the poet moves from the last of the verse poems to the *Illuminations*. In these prose poems the child and his smouldering rebellion ('il suait d'obéissance'), which were presented in detailed physical terms in 'Les Poètes de sept ans', are transformed into a universal statement with infinite reverberations, 'De petits enfants étouffent des malédictions le long des rivières'; and the mother, no longer localised and in the likeness of a particular person, becomes a 'misérable femme de drame, quelque part dans le monde'. The body itself is treated as an aesthetic object, and is referred to in sensuous but general terms as 'chairs superbes', idealised as a 'corps adoré', seen imaginatively as 'un fruit pendu dans le verger', experienced as something completely new, 'Un nouveau corps amoureux', or (in 'Barbare') broken into 'les formes, les sueurs, les chevelures et les yeux, flottant' — separate and 'floating' elements, yet skilfully organised into one of the most enigmatic and haunting scenes in a continuing drama.

That Rimbaud should have been able, in progressing from the *Poésies* through the 1872 verse poems to the *Illuminations*, to purify and change completely both the substance and the form of his poetry is a remarkable achievement, all the more so when one considers the extent and the intensity of his preoccupation with the immediate, the physical and the concrete in the early verse poems.

5

LAST AND NEW VERSES

In 1870, Rimbaud had on three occasions escaped briefly from home, but his most important 'flight' was in September 1871, when he went to Paris at the invitation of Verlaine. He had taken with him 'Le Bateau ivre', written expressly for the visit, and several other poems, but these failed to win for him the 'dazzling entry' into the literary world, the success and the fame, which Delahaye, and he himself, had anticipated. 'Les gens de Paris' could not appreciate the originality of his poetry, and they reacted strongly against his insolent behaviour and his unconventional dress, 'débraillé comme un étudiant'. The six months in Paris yielded, on the human side, the notorious homosexual relationship with Verlaine, ten years his senior, and, on the literary side, about twenty poems, mostly *dizains* and sonnets, which he wrote during the winter of 1871–2 while he was a member of the Cercle zutique. The Zutistes – so called because they said *Zut!* to the bourgeois and his values – included, in addition to Verlaine and Rimbaud, Charles Cros, Léon Valade, Camille Pelletan, Germain Nouveau, Jean Richepin, Raoul Ponchon, the composer Cabaner, and the photographer Carjat. Their meetings, which took place at the Hôtel des Étrangers in the Latin Quarter, are 'recorded' in a thirty-page book, the *Album zutique*,[1] a collection of parodies and pastiches, mainly of the Parnassians – in particular of François Coppée. Some of these are bawdy, some witty; a few are anti-clerical, and at times they are accompanied by amusing or obscene sketches. None of Rimbaud's contributions is of great importance, but the most interesting is a long poem, 'Les Remembrances du vieillard idiot', which, although ostensibly a parody of Coppée, reveals in a much cruder form than in 'Les Poètes de sept ans' the sexual obsessions of an adolescent.

After his return to Charleville and before his departure in July with Verlaine to Belgium and then to London, Rimbaud wrote sixteen verse poems which occupy a special place in his life and work. They represent a period of relative calm between the disillusionment of the time in Paris and the beginning of a more prolonged and turbulent phase of the relationship with Verlaine, and, coming midway between the early verse poems and the *Illuminations*, they correspond to a new, experimental stage in his work. Originally some of them were published in the first edition of the *Illuminations*; but recently editors have placed them together as a separate group between the *Poésies* and the *Illuminations*, some giving them the title *Vers nouveaux et chansons*, and others *Derniers vers*. The first suggests the newness and the more lyrical quality of these song-like poems compared with the *Poésies*; and the second indicates that they are Rimbaud's last poems in verse before he began to experiment, in the *Illuminations*, with the *poème en prose*.

The meditativeness and relative calm of these 1872 verse poems are unusual, though not unique, in his work, which, like his life, is characterised by incessant movement. For Mallarmé, he was a 'passant considérable'; Verlaine called him 'l'homme aux semelles de vent'; more recently, Saint-John Perse referred to him as 'ce poète de l'ellipse et du bond', and René Char summed him up in one word, 'rapidité'. The expression 'une chasse spirituelle', the presumed title of one of the 'lost' manuscripts, is frequently used to describe not only certain poems, such as 'Aube', but the general tenor of his work, or, as he himself expresses it in 'Les Sœurs de charité':

Rêves ou Promenades
Immenses, à travers les nuits de Vérité . . .

Movement, real or imagined, linear or dialectical, is a major feature of his career, but it varies in tempo and rhythm, from the 'terrible célérité' of 'Génie' to 'les arrêts de la vie' of 'Départ'. There are whole poems which are 'static', poems of physical tiredness and contentment, such as 'Au Cabaret-Vert' and 'La Maline', suspended, as it were, in time between journeys; and, again on the physical plane, there are poems in which movement and repose alternate, as in 'Ma Bohème', or are combined, as in the 'petit wagon rose' of 'Rêvé pour l'hiver'. On a higher plane there are moments of contemplation and deep insight, such as 'Larme' and 'Mémoire' (two of the 1872 texts); on yet another plane there is, in 'Veillées', 'le repos éclairé, ni fièvre, ni langueur', a poised state, at once physical and spiritual, where, in a brief instant before reality intervenes, the poet receives not only illumination but 'la vie'.

In the *Vers nouveaux*, there is none of the brash rebelliousness, or exclamatory over-emphasis, of the adolescent. Disillusionment and solitude have changed Rimbaud's perception of external phenomena and of his inner being. His senses have been quickened and made more acutely responsive, particularly to sounds. The centre of his poetry is no longer a physical presence (his own), as in 'Au Cabaret-Vert', but the spirit, which is vigilant and receptive to every sound and murmur. This turning inwards is evident in the first poem, 'Qu'est-ce pour nous, mon cœur, que les nappes de sang', where, to initiate a reflective dialogue, he addresses his heart, and in another poem, 'L'Éternité', where he appeals to his 'âme sentinelle' — traditional literary devices, but used with naturalness and conviction.

The change of emphasis is particularly marked in the imagery which is now mainly auditory rather than visual. The sound of the river and of the wind dominates in 'La Rivière de Cassis', where one *hears* 'les passions mortes des chevaliers errants' and where the 'cris sévères' of the crows (heard before in 'Les Corbeaux') have become in a striking image a 'vraie/Et bonne voix d'anges'. Verbs of sound introduce each of the poems: 'Le loup criait sous les feuilles', and, a more original example, 'Entends comme brame'; while in 'Fêtes de la patience', the opposed themes of patience and impatience are announced by an opposition of sounds — the dying notes of a 'maladif hallali' and the winged 'chansons spirituelles' — and by lines where the meaning is expressed by discreetly alliterating vowels and consonants. In 'Bruxelles' the singing of a 'blanche Irlandaise' to the accompaniment of a guitar is heard against a background of jargoning birds and the chatter of children, and in 'Fêtes de la faim' the whole world, the scene of the poet's hunger, is resonant with sound, from the 'pré des sons' to the 'azur sonneur'.

The most interesting and original examples of this preoccupation with sounds occur in 'Âge d'or', the last of a sequence of four poems which compose 'Fêtes de la patience'. This lyric is a remarkable blending of speech and music, with first a solo voice, then a chorus of voices, now speaking, now singing to the poet, who is himself alternately listener and participator. In previous poems, like 'Voyelles' and 'Le Bateau ivre', Rimbaud had tested and stretched to fresh limits the visual possibilities of language; he is now exploiting in a half-playful, half-ironic way sound values and auditory effects. At times, sounds appear merely to suggest or generate sounds, as for example in 'Bruxelles':

> Quelles
> Troupes d'oiseaux! ô iaio, iaio! ...

and

> — La Juliette, ça rappelle l'Henriette,

but in 'Âge d'or' (and in other poems in this group) the intention, though apparently light-hearted, is serious; and the grammar, syntax, and sound patterns are interwoven as if to trace, and mimic, the involvement of human relationships, as well as those in nature. A voice, addressing the poet in speech and song, explains:

> Reconnais ce tour
> Si gai, si facile:
> Ce n'est qu'onde, flore,
> Et c'est ta famille!
>
> Puis elle chante. Ô
> Si gai, si facile,
> Et visible à l'œil nu ...
> —Je chante avec elle, —
>
> Reconnais ce tour
> Si gai, si facile,
> Ce n'est qu'onde, flore,
> Et c'est ta famille! ... etc.

Several meanings of the keyword 'tour' — a rotation, twist or turn; a circular shape or movement; a form of expression or figure of speech — are suggested in the turning and pirouetting of the ten stanzas and the rondeau-like movement. This delicate intricacy is also apparent in the images, such as 'onde' and 'flore', which convey visually and musically the all-embracing nature of the family; and again in the single letter 'Ô' which is at once a visual and an auditory image, a figure (a 'tour') and a musical note.

The family, and relationships of various kinds, past and present, human, religious, symbolic and legendary, are touched upon in most of these poems. In 'Qu'est-ce pour nous, mon cœur, que les nappes de sang', Rimbaud thinks of his 'friends' and 'brothers', fellow revolutionaries, and in 'Bonne pensée du matin' of the workers, those who build and construct. 'Michel et Christine' is an idyll which ends with a symbolic tableau of man and wife, and Christ; 'Jeune ménage' is a parody of the household and life of the newly-weds, Verlaine and his child-wife Mathilde; and 'Comédie de la soif' is an evocation of the poet's ancestors, of contemporaries and friends, and of legendary figures. But Rimbaud gaily derides or brutally rejects all relationships. Nothing they offer can satisfy him, and, paradoxically, he remains free and at the same time imprisoned by his insatiable appetites.

These poems or *romances* represent, as Rimbaud was to say later when he quoted them in *Une Saison en enfer*, his 'farewell to the world', the world of bourgeois society and futile literary discussions. For the moment, however, he turns to familiar landscapes and to nature, and in 'Bannières de mai' he declares:

> À toi, Nature, je me rends;
> Et ma faim et toute ma soif.

Those two lines may suggest that nature is a maternal symbol, but Rimbaud's contempt for Musset's cry 'Ô nature! ô ma mère!' in 'Souvenir' should make us wary of identifying his attitude with that of any of the Romantic poets.[2] His 'hunger' and 'thirst', which are the themes of two complementary poems, 'Fêtes de la faim' and 'Comédie de la soif', are virile, un-Romantic appetites. He sees nature not as a friend, confidante, or mother-figure, to whom he appeals for help or consolation, but as an elemental force to which he returns to renew and purify his poetic vision.

Among poems that express frustration, self-criticism, a desire for freedom, and extreme suffering, there are also moments of ecstasy and enraptured discovery, as in 'L'Éternité':

> Elle est retrouvée.
> Quoi? — L'Éternité.

> C'est la mer allée
> Avec le soleil.

One is reminded of the English metaphysical poet Henry Vaughan's 'I saw Eternity the other night/Like a great *Ring* of pure and endless light'; but the comparison only emphasises the un-metaphysical and un-mystical nature of Rimbaud's poem, the unique simplicity of a vision in which eternity is something as natural as this meeting and 'going together' of sea and sun. In other poems, 'Larme' and 'Michel et Christine', nature, or rather changes in nature — the commotion of a storm, variations in temperature and in the light and colours of a landscape — produce a sequence of fresh poetic visions. In 'Larme', for example, the heat of the afternoon, 'tiède et vert', and the sultry sky suggest an Eastern country, where water becomes a 'liqueur d'or'. With the storm the sky changes, and the vision also:

> Ce furent des pays noirs, des lacs, des perches,
> Des colonnades sous la nuit bleue, des gares.

The final image comes as the wind changes the scene again:

> Le vent, du ciel, jetait des glaçons aux mares.

A similar technique is used in 'Mémoire', the most important of this group of poems, which Rimbaud wrote in the spring of 1872. In his work it stands midway between the *Poésies* and the *Illuminations*, and in his life also this poem occupies a central place. Here he is no longer the adolescent aggressively displaying his talents, but the *voyant* who is seeing, feeling, and using words in a new way.

In both form and content this is a more complex poem than 'Les Poètes de sept ans', 'Voyelles', or 'Le Bateau ivre'. Whereas those appear to have been composed line by line, stanza by stanza, 'Mémoire' is an organic whole which has been formed in the depths of the poet's personality. Instead of striving to capture visions from the extremities of an imagined world, as in 'Le Bateau ivre', he is now receiving them from 'l'eau claire'. The stanza form and the alexandrine, although superficially orthodox, reflect this deepening of experience. Some of the formal rules are obeyed, but the metre has been changed from within. By weakening and varying the place of the caesura,

by an increased use of enjambement, and by using the feminine
rhyme throughout, Rimbaud has completely transformed the
classical metre, making it an exceptionally supple and fluid
means of expression.

MÉMOIRE

I

L'eau claire; comme le sel des larmes d'enfance,
L'assaut au soleil des blancheurs des corps de femmes,
la soie, en foule et de lys pur, des oriflammes
sous les murs dont quelque pucelle eut la défense;

L'ébat des anges; —Non . . . le courant d'or en marche,
meut ses bras, noirs, et lourds, et frais surtout d'herbe. Elle
sombre, ayant le Ciel bleu pour ciel-de-lit, appelle
pour rideaux l'ombre de la colline et de l'arche.

II

Eh! l'humide carreau tend ses bouillons limpides!
L'eau meuble d'or pâle et sans fond les couches prêtes.
Les robes vertes et déteintes des fillettes
font les saules, d'où sautent les oiseaux sans brides.

Plus pure qu'un louis, jaune et chaude paupière
le souci d'eau —ta foi conjugale, ô l'Épouse! —
au midi prompt, de son terne miroir, jalouse
au ciel gris de chaleur la Sphère rose et chère.

III

Madame se tient trop debout dans la prairie
prochaine où neigent les fils du travail; l'ombrelle
aux doigts; foulant l'ombelle; trop fière pour elle;
des enfants lisant dans la verdure fleurie

leur livre de maroquin rouge! Hélas, Lui, comme
mille anges blancs qui se séparent sur la route,
s'éloigne par delà la montagne! Elle, toute
froide, et noire, court! après le départ de l'homme!

IV

Regret des bras épais et jeunes d'herbe pure!
Or des lunes d'avril au cœur du saint lit! Joie

des chantiers riverains à l'abandon, en proie
aux soirs d'août qui faisaient germer ces pourritures!

Qu'elle pleure à présent sous les remparts! l'haleine
des peupliers d'en haut est pour la seule brise.
Puis, c'est la nappe, sans reflets, sans source, grise:
un vieux, dragueur, dans sa barque immobile, peine.

V

Jouet de cet œil d'eau morne, je n'y puis prendre,
Ô canot immobile! Oh! bras trop courts! ni l'une
ni l'autre fleur: ni la jaune qui m'importune,
là; ni la bleue, amie à l'eau couleur de cendre.

Ah! la poudre des saules qu'une aile secoue!
Les roses des roseaux dès longtemps dévorées!
Mon canot, toujours fixe; et sa chaîne tirée
Au fond de cet œil d'eau sans bords, —à quelle boue?

In the first stanza, the sensation of whiteness is obtained by
subtler means than in 'Voyelles', where the technique is 'linear',
and the effect cumulative. Throughout 'Mémoire' there is a
delicate interplay, not just horizontally but also vertically, and
the opening stanza mingles the whiteness of clear water, salt,
tears, bodies of women, silk, and a lily, with the yellow and gold
of the sun and the oriflammes' red and gold. In the same way an
intricate and dynamic verbal pattern is formed by an association
of ideas — clarity, sadness, childhood, war, eroticism, purity,
royalty, virginity. This stanza, which conveys the movement and
the very texture of water (cf. 'la soie des mers' in 'Barbare')
seen in the light of the sun, creates a shock of pleasurable surprise, and we recognise that Rimbaud is doing something quite
different from recollecting in the Romantic manner, as Lamartine and Musset each did in their poems entitled 'Souvenir'.
For him, memory is not an intellectual activity, a recalling of
the past like the plot of a novel, but an alert interest which
suddenly focuses on moments of emotional significance, or on
the unexpected appearance in the mind of thoughts and images
from the unconscious. The river with its surface-play of varying
lights and reflections, and its sombre and mysterious depths,
is the perfect image to convey this dual aspect of memory.
Many critics who regard memory as a logical process have

related the people, the landscape and the flora of 'Mémoire' to Charleville and the Ardennes. The river is thought to be the Meuse; the sun and the woman the poet's father and mother; and the drama in the third section, concluding with 'le départ de l'homme', either Captain Rimbaud's final separation from Madame Rimbaud, or one of the flights of the poet himself from his mother. This instant 'key' is, however, an oversimplification, and takes no account of numerous linguistic ambiguities, notably of the possible meanings, or stresses, that critics have attributed to 'Lui' in line 21, namely, Captain Rimbaud, the husband who abandons his wife; Captain Rimbaud, the father who abandons his children; Rimbaud himself who wishes to leave his mother and Charleville; or the sun setting behind the mountain. The frequency of indefinite and general terms, such as 'l'eau ... quelque pucelle ... l'Épouse ... Madame ... des enfants ... Lui ... Elle ... l'homme ... la jaune ... la bleue ...' invites the reader to approach the poem in a less reductive and more imaginative way. 'Mémoire' works simultaneously on several levels, so that 'Lui' and 'Elle' can be taken as real or mythical people; as a real or imagined sun and river; as symbols of life — the elements, fire and water. The variety and divergence of the interpretations are evidence not of any confusion in the poem but, on the ohter hand, of its complexity and evocative power.

The main symbols, water and the river for the woman, sun and light for the man, suggest that Rimbaud is expressing a universal or archetypal theme of desire, union and separation, rather than (or perhaps as well as) a conflict between identifiable people. The idea of conflict (explicit in 'assaut' and 'défense') is present in a pure elemental form in the opening stanza, and is developed up to the end of the fourth section, when the introduction of the 'je' (the poet himself) brings in childhood, which has already been touched on in the first, third and fifth stanzas. But the theme which embraces all the planes and profundities of the poem is the theme announced in the title: 'Mémoire'. This includes conflict and childhood at both a personal and a universal level; landscapes and river scenes, at once recognisable, impressionistic and symbolical; the river, which could be the Meuse flowing between Charleville and Mézières and is at the same time the symbol of woman and of memory itself — the stream of the conscious and unconscious mind.

Everything is interrelated and, as the river's clear water changes to dark depths, leads in the final scene to the desolation of the poet —a desolation that was foreshadowed in the opening line, 'L'eau claire; comme le sel des larmes d'enfance'. This is the conclusion to the drama that has been enacted in the preceding stanzas. Each comparison between the river and the poet, its arms 'épais et jeunes d'herbe pure' and his 'trop courts'; its freedom and his immobility; and, in another dimension, the movement of time ('les roses des roseaux dès longtemps dévorées!'), all these underline his helplessness. There is a particular irony in the position of the *voyant* imprisoned by an eye, 'cet œil d'eau morne', 'cet œil d'eau sans bords' (more sinister than 'les yeux horribles des pontons'), and by a force which he can neither see nor understand.

In a psychological examination of the poem other aspects would be stressed, such as the sexual symbolism of the 'œil d'eau', and the biological symbolism of the mud that holds fast the chain of the boat. The setting of the conjugal bed scene in the bed of the river (in section I) would also, no doubt, be interpreted as the poet's desire for the death of his parents. The many interpretations that can be discovered beneath the luminous surface of this major poem are some indication of the disturbing crisis through which Rimbaud was passing. They are also a measure of the enrichment of his genius —an enrichment which, in the *Illuminations*, finds expression in the original form of the prose poem.

The *Vers nouveaux et chansons* are exceptional in Rimbaud's work not only in their imagery, auditory rather than visual, and in their themes of human and other relationships (two aspects that have so far received little or no attention from critics); they are also exceptional in their verse forms and versification. In these new poems there are none of the traditional forms of poetry. Stanzas are still used, but they vary in length from two to ten lines, and the length of the stanza itself is not always constant within the same poem — in 'Bannières de mai' the opening stanza has ten lines while the other two have eight. The number of syllables in the line also varies, from four to twelve, and the *impair* (which Verlaine had exploited with delicate skill) is used with from five to eleven syllables and in ingenious combinations in eleven of the poems — notably in 'Fêtes de la faim'. Except in 'Qu'est-ce pour nous, mon cœur, que les nappes de sang' and in 'Mémoire', where the alexandrine is used, the rhyme schemes are frequently irregular, and the rhymes, according to the rules of versification, are usually 'imperfect' or 'defective'. A fine discrimination and delight are apparent in this deliberate and constructive misuse of rhyme, for Rimbaud breaks the rules with as much skill and inventiveness as he had previously displayed in obeying and mastering them. He takes especial pleasure in doing so precisely because they had acquired, since the seventeenth century, an almost moral authority. Any departure from them, particularly as regards the *consonne d'appui*, was judged, by Dumarsais, Quicherat and Banville, to be reprehensible, blameworthy, and the gravest of faults.

Théodore de Banville, in his *Petit traité de poésie française* (which appeared the same year as the *Vers nouveaux et chansons* were composed), had stated that the *consonne d'appui* was as necessary to a poet as an arm or a leg and that without it neither rhyme nor poetry was possible, and in the chapter, 'Encore la Rime', under the heading 'Licences poétiques', he categorically declared: 'Il n'y en a pas.'[3] But Rimbaud, now totally opposed to the Parnassian master he had once admired, demands every poetic licence and complete freedom in dealing with consonants, vowels, assonance, and in particular with the tyrannies of rhyme. For the most part, he reduces rhyme to assonance, and frequently to assonance in its weakest form. Thus, in 'L'Éternité' he uses words with the same vowel, but no supporting consonant, as a 'rhyme' at the end of a line ('retrouvée', 'éternité' and 'allée'/'aveu' and 'feu'), or words which have a different vowel but pronounced consonants (sometimes one only) that are the same ('sentinelle' and 'nulle'/'seules' and 's'exhale'/'élans' and 'selon'). Occasionally he does not rhyme at all, as in 'Le loup criait sous les feuilles' ('fruits' and 'haie'), and at the end of 'Entends comme brame' ('Allemagne' and 'tristement'). Examples of all these 'defective' rhymes (and some *rimes riches*) can be found in 'Âge d'or', where, as in the stanzas quoted on p. 39, Rimbaud seems to be rhyming for the eye as well as for the ear ('facile' and 'famille'), and also to be aiming at effects of modulation between vowels rather than any strict conformity of sound ('tour' and 'flore'/'Ô' and 'nu'/'château' and 'tu'). These unexpected sonorities — which are a fresh aspect of his work — both surprise and please the ear by their nearness to, and finely calculated departure from, a known rule and pattern of sound.

In his article 'Arthur Rimbaud' in *Les Poètes maudits*, Verlaine mentioned some of the main technical features in the *Vers nouveaux et chansons*: 'assonances', 'mots vagues', 'phrases enfantines ou populaires'.[4] These are, in fact, devices he himself had used in the *Fêtes galantes* and *Romances sans paroles*, and which, along with others, such as the use of the *impair*, he advocated in his poem, 'Art poétique'. It is therefore natural that he should have appreciated their virtues and described the poems as 'prodiges de ténuité', for in them he recognised the influence his own technique and practice had undoubtedly had on his friend. But Rimbaud, while expressing his solitude and the bitterness of recent experience, is never plaintive or sentimental, and even in the most subjective and child-like of these songs there is, as can be seen in the opening stanza of 'Chanson de la plus haute tour', firmness, clarity and a sharp edge to the feeling:

> Oisive jeunesse
> À tout asservie
> Par délicatesse
> J'ai perdu ma vie.
> Ah! Que le temps vienne
> Où les cœurs s'éprennent.

In technical matters and versification, and notably in his treatment of rhyme, that grossly over-valued 'bijou d'un sou', he is decisive and revolutionary. Whereas Verlaine maintained that rhyme of some kind was 'un mal nécessaire', and that without it poetry was not possible, Rimbaud, after abusing it to good purpose in the *Vers nouveaux et chansons*, finally dispensed with it altogether in 'Marine' and 'Mouvement', two poems (now included in the *Illuminations*) which are considered by many critics to be the first completely 'free verse' poems in the French language.

6

ILLUMINATIONS

The problem that has complicated and distorted the study of Rimbaud's writings has been one of chronology. It is still not known whether *Une Saison en enfer* is the last work he wrote, or whether all, or some, of the *Illuminations* were written after it had been completed.

In the first edition of the *Œuvres complètes* (1898), the following order was adopted: *Poésies, Les Illuminations, Autres Illuminations,* and *Une Saison en enfer,* and for over fifty years *Une Saison en enfer* was generally considered to be the final work. That order seemed natural and logical because it showed, on the literary plane, an evolution from verse poems, through highly original prose poems, to poetic prose and prose statement; and it was paralleled, on the human plane, by a movement from a world of theory and symbols to a world of practicalities and action. It had the shape of a drama: exposition, climax, dénouement. Moreover, in *Une Saison en enfer* Rimbaud reviews his past achievements, both literary and human, and appears to reject them; and in the concluding section, significantly entitled 'Adieu', he prepares to grapple with 'rugged reality'. This adieu, which can be read as Rimbaud's renunciation of and farewell to literature, seemed at one time to be confirmed by the legend that, in a dramatic gesture, he burned all the copies of *Une Saison en enfer*. These, however, except for a few sent to friends, were discovered by chance in 1901 by M. Léon Losseau, a Belgian bibliophile, in the attic of the Brussels firm, Poot & Co., where they had been printed, and where they had remained unclaimed because Rimbaud had not been able to pay the printer's bill. The account of the discovery was not published until 1915, and it passed unnoticed during the war, but even when the story of the *auto-da-fé* was disproved, the legend of the 'last work' died hard. Eventually, however, as critics began to question the traditional order, the *Illuminations* became the main focus of interest and scholarship.

In 1948 H. de Bouillane de Lacoste published a thesis, *Rimbaud et le problème des 'Illuminations'*, in which he sought to prove that the *Illuminations* were composed between 1873 and 1875, that is, after *Une Saison en enfer*. Despite the fragility of his hypothesis, based on a study of Rimbaud's erratic handwriting, and on one selected statement by the unreliable Verlaine, his conclusion was widely accepted and, in most recent editions of the *Œuvres complètes*, the *Illuminations* have been placed as the last poetic work. This new order, however, is no more certain than the traditional one, and no critic would be so dogmatic as to affirm that all the *Illuminations* were written before, or that all were written after, *Une Saison en enfer*. Indeed, the state of the manuscripts, the handwriting, the internal evidence and what we know of Rimbaud's life suggest that these prose poems were written sporadically during the period from 1872 to 1875, the majority before, a few after, *Une Saison en enfer*, and some while he was composing his 'farewell' to literature.[1]

The chronological problem, which for a time became an obsession with critics, appears less important now than it once did, except to the exegetist who wishes to situate a text and to talk with some degree of certainty about a poet's evolution. Perhaps the most helpful approach is that suggested by Camus in *L'Homme révolté*: 'The order in which his two great works were produced is of no importance ... every artist knows, and with the absolute certainty that comes from a life's experience, that Rimbaud carried within him the *Saison* and the *Illuminations* at the same time. If he wrote them one after the other, he agonised over them simultaneously.'[2] Camus has, of course, simplified the problem by taking the *Illuminations* to be, like *Une Saison en enfer*, a coherent and completed *œuvre*, whereas they are a series of fragments, with no discernible plan and no definite conclusion.

Most of the poems in the *Illuminations* have been interpreted or decoded; but there are still large areas, both aesthetic and factual, that remain obscure, even hermetic. Little is known about their background, origin, and composition; and up to now it has proved impossible to set them in a precise context. As far as we know (a cautionary expression which should accompany most statements about this problem), Rimbaud, who

dated his early verse poems and *Une Saison en enfer*, did not date
any of these 'superb fragments'. He did not arrange them in any
particular order, and he did not even know if they would be
published. It has not yet been discovered exactly how the manuscripts, after being in the hands of Verlaine and his brother-in-
law Charles de Sivry, eventually reached Gustave Kahn, the
editor of the Symbolist review *La Vogue*, which, in 1886,
published all of them except the five so-called *Autres Illuminations* — 'Fairy', 'Guerre', 'Génie', 'Jeunesse', 'Solde'.[3] At this
time, Rimbaud had become a trader in Abyssinia and knew
nothing of the publication. *La Vogue* equally knew little about
him, for in the comments that accompanied the poems he is
referred to as 'the late Arthur Rimbaud' and 'the equivocal
and glorious deceased'. Later the same year the *Illuminations*
were published by *La Vogue* in volume form, with a preface by
Verlaine in which he explained: 'Le mot *Illuminations* est
anglais et veut dire gravures coloriées, — *coloured plates*: c'est
même le sous-titre que M. Rimbaud avait donné à son manu-
scrit.' The statement is definite enough, but no mention has
been found in Rimbaud's work of any such general title or
subtitle. Delahaye, however, refers in *Rimbaud. L'artiste et l'être
moral* to *Photographie des temps passés*, which may be the *Illuminations*. This title certainly suggests their visual, objective nature;
but the word 'photographie' implies a mechanical quality which
is foreign to them, and 'passés' is an inappropriate term to use
about poems that constantly seek to evoke the future.

Even if Rimbaud did not choose the title, the word *Illuminations* is unusually appropriate, for its different meanings, from
the physical to the spiritual, cover many aspects of these short
prose poems. 'Les Ponts', 'Mystique' and 'Fleurs', for example,
have the sharpness and clarity of coloured plates or illuminated
manuscripts; others, such as 'Veillées', 'Nocturne vulgaire',
and 'Scènes', are more like controlled hallucinations or waking
dreams, in which the interplay of light, colours and sounds
creates fresh contexts and perspectives; and some, notably
'Conte', 'Royauté', 'Ornières' and 'Aube', are illuminating insights about Rimbaud himself, the duality of human nature, and
man's spiritual quest. But the *Illuminations*, a sustained if not
systematic application of the *voyant* theory, are 'accessible à
tous les sens' and appeal not only to the visual but to all the

senses. They are essentially dynamic, and some are so varied and complex that they could be placed in each of the above three categories, while some could not be confined within any of them. Rimbaud's own terms, 'parade sauvage', 'opéra fabuleux', 'comédie humaine', indicate other and wider aspects of these moments of inspired insight.

A recent study by Nathaniel Wing, who sees them as self-sufficient verbal systems, begins with the following paradoxical statement: 'A reading of Rimbaud's *Illuminations* must first account for an absence', by which he means the absence for him of any reference to reality.[4] But the *Illuminations* are, like Baudelaire's conception of a modern form of 'pure art', at once objective and subjective, and they include both 'le monde extérieur à l'artiste' and 'l'artiste lui-même'; in other words, there is within them a presence, the presence of reality and of Rimbaud himself. He may seem isolated from the world and indifferent to any audience, but in fact we are the public he confronts and attacks, whether indirectly as in 'Après le déluge', or directly as in 'Vies', where he asks: 'Qu'est mon néant, auprès de la stupeur qui vous attend?' As in the early poems, and in *Une Saison en enfer*, there is the same urgent need to communicate, but the emotions are more controlled and they are, for the most part, expressed in general and symbolic terms.

In studying the *Illuminations*, further differences of opinion have occurred about the order in which the 'fragments' should be placed. Editions occasionally end with 'Départ', sometimes with 'Solde', and more frequently with 'Génie' – all possible conclusions. There is, however, agreement that they begin with 'Après le déluge'. We do not know if Rimbaud himself would have placed this poem first, but it has appeared in that position in all editions since 1886, when Félix Fénéon prepared the manuscripts, 'a risky pack of cards', as he termed them, for publication in *La Vogue*. 'Après le déluge' announces some of the main themes of protest that are developed in subsequent poems: protest against nature, religion, bourgeois ideas about childhood and education, a materialistic culture and civilisation. Above all, it is animated by Rimbaud's central theme, the alternation and conflict between forces of destruction and creation; and it contains many of his essential stylistic features: vivid images, dynamic and rapidly changing rhythms, swift transitions from short sentences to sustained rhetoric, abruptness and finality of utterance.

APRÈS LE DÉLUGE

Aussitôt que l'idée du Déluge se fut rassise,

Un lièvre s'arrêta dans les sainfoins et les clochettes mouvantes et dit sa prière à l'arc-en-ciel à travers la toile de l'araignée.

Oh! les pierres précieuses qui se cachaient, —les fleurs qui regardaient déjà.

Dans la grande rue sale les étals se dressèrent, et l'on tira les barques vers la mer étagée là-haut comme sur les gravures.

Le sang coula, chez Barbe-Bleue, —aux abattoirs, —dans les cirques, où le sceau de Dieu blêmit les fenêtres. Le sang et le lait coulèrent.

Les castors bâtirent, les "mazagrans" fumèrent dans les estaminets.

Dans la grande maison de vitres encore ruisselante les enfants en deuil regardèrent les merveilleuses images.

Une porte claqua, — et sur la place du hameau, l'enfant tourna ses bras, compris des girouettes et des coqs des clochers de partout, sous l'éclatante giboulée.

Madame*** établit un piano dans les Alpes. La messe et les premières communions se célébrèrent aux cent mille autels de la cathédrale.

Les caravanes partirent. Et le Splendide-Hôtel fut bâti dans le chaos de glaces et de nuit du pôle.

Depuis lors, la Lune entendit les chacals piaulant par les déserts de thym, —et les églogues en sabots grognant dans le verger. Puis, dans la futaie violette, bourgeonnante, Eucharis me dit que c'était le printemps.

— Sourds, étang, — Écume, roule sur le pont et par-dessus les bois ; — draps noirs et orgues, — éclairs et tonnerre, — montez et roulez ; — Eaux et tristesses, montez et relevez les Déluges.

Car depuis qu'ils se sont dissipés, — oh les pierres précieuses s'enfouissant, et les fleurs ouvertes ! — c'est un ennui !

et la Reine, la Sorcière qui allume sa braise dans le pot de
terre, ne voudra jamais nous raconter ce qu'elle sait, et que
nous ignorons.

From the title to the conclusion, Rimbaud's treatment of the
Flood is original in every detail. Most artists, whether painters
or poets, have followed the Bible account, and have depicted,
often with melodramatic variations, the actual Flood. They
have shown the opening of the heavens, the darkened sky rent
by thunder and lightning, the devastation of nature, the destruction of mankind, and finally the Ark lifted by the rising
waters to a safe resting-place on a high mountain. One thinks,
for example, of the writings and drawings by Leonardo da
Vinci of waves and the Deluge, and, nearer to Rimbaud's time,
paintings of the Flood by Géricault, Gustave Doré and John
Martin (Turner, on the other hand, is an important exception,
for he painted a *Morning after the Deluge*).[5] Hugo's epic poem
'Le Déluge' and Vigny's 'Le Déluge' are also grandiose develop-
ments of the Bible story. All these representations of the Flood
convey the same message, which Vigny expressed concisely as
'L'homme était méchant.'

Rimbaud's starting-point is not the Flood, but the moment
after the Flood, when everything appears normal again, and
human beings and animals are resuming their customary
activities. By comparison with Hugo and Vigny, Rimbaud's
illumination may appear an anticlimax, with everything –
animals, people and objects – on a small scale, like a child's
picture compared with that of an old master. This effect is
partly the result of the change from the conventional verse
forms of Romanticism to the flexibility of a modern prose
poem; but the main difference is that, in 'Après le déluge', the
perspectives have changed. Instead of the gradual and continuous development of a narrative or scene, there is a series of
images, some related, others juxtaposed. Swiftly moving sentences take the reader from a single figure, an animal at prayer,
to the communicants at the hundred thousand altars; from
the village square to the Alps and the Pole; from the separate
images of water – the sea, the streaming window panes, the
sparkling shower of rain –to the poet's impassioned invocation
in which all the waters are gathered up. This is not a story

retold, but a fresh and personal vision, in which man is not
merely 'méchant' but spiritually blind. It is a vision in which a
second flood — that of the poet's anger — is the real climax. It
is not the spectacle that concerns Rimbaud but what lies behind it, *l'idée* du Déluge'. As soon as the waters had subsided,
the meaning of the Flood as God's punishment had faded from
the minds of men. Saved from disaster, they began again, as if
nothing had happened, the routine of their existence.

The image of the hare praying to the rainbow is appropriate
because the hare is an archetypal symbol of existence, resur-
rection and fertility.[6] In some mythologies it is closely associated
with Noah and the Flood, and in an American-Indian legend,
a hare instead of a dove is sent forth to see if the waters have
abated. On a first reading it seems a beautiful image, standing out
like a figure in an illuminated manuscript, psalter or *Livre de
chasse* as if to announce the freshness and wonder of a purified
world. But the context, and what we know of Rimbaud's work
as a whole, suggest that the picture of the hare is sentimental,
even pretty-pretty, perhaps in derisive imitation of La Fontaine's
fable 'Le Chat, la belette, et le petit lapin', in which Janot, the
little rabbit, 'était allé faire à l'Aurore, sa cour/Parmi le thym et
la rosée'.[7] The image is, in fact, both sentimental and ironic,
and the hare will, like the worshippers at the 'cent mille autels',
and all else, be swept away. The main point is, however, that by
placing first an animal praying rather than a human being
(Noah in the Genesis account) Rimbaud emphasises man's in-
gratitude, and his indifference both to the beauty of the earth and
to the meaning of the rainbow, God's covenant in the sky.

In an apparently artless way, Rimbaud constructs a complex
world in which there are fairy-tale and biblical elements and a
classical reference, as well as the realism of everyday existence.
At the beginning and at the end of the text, material things —
precious stones and flowers — behave normally: the jewels are
first hiding then burying themselves (perhaps to escape from
man's greed), while the flowers, after looking around, become
fully open. Within this framework, there is a sequence of unrelated human activities, commerce, trade, building, culture, religion, exploration and tourism expressed in symbolic form. In
the middle there are children in mourning followed by the
isolated image of a child, who is understood only by the weather-

vanes and weather-cocks because he, like them, is turning round to find his bearings. But all directions lead to the absurdity of bourgeois culture, represented by 'Madame***' and her piano in the Alps, and to the kind of progress symbolised by the ironically named 'Splendide' Hotel.

In this world after the Flood there is nothing new. Nature remains the same with the predictable regularity of her changing seasons. The announcement by Eucharis, the most beautiful of Calypso's nymphs, that spring has come, seen by some commentators as a 'magical' moment, is for Rimbaud the abhorrent sign of the monotony of nature's self-renewal.[8] He replies by invoking the waters and their accompaniment of thunder and lightning to rise and purify the earth again. Because it is all so dull and repetitious, such an 'ennui', this picture-book world has to be swept away. The balancing of verbs and nouns, and the biblical-like repetition of 'et', give force and authority to a rhetorical passage which is itself a deluge of controlled rage. In the conclusion, the poet's anger is mainly directed at nature, the Queen and Sorceress, who holds the closely guarded secret of life and fertility which the poet envies, but also despises. His contempt is concentrated in an image of the earth reduced to the size of an earthen pot or witch's cauldron, 'pot de terre' (cf. Laforgue's image, 'La Terre, elle est ronde comme un pot-au-feu' in 'Petites misères d'août'). The revolt which Rimbaud had expressed in his verse poems (notably in 'L'Orgie parisienne'), against man's corruption and the ravaging of 'La Nature verte', has become in 'Après le déluge' a revolt against nature and the human condition. The imagined destruction of our world is necessary so that Rimbaud can be free to create his visionary world, in which things and people will live a new and purer life.

We are led into this visionary world immediately after 'Après le déluge' through five short poems under the general title 'Enfance'. Here things and people do not behave normally, and they serve no utilitarian end. Their only function is to exist as poetic elements in a poem; and it is precisely because they have been detached from links with real life that they can live in a different way. Thus, the child has no parents, the waves of the sea no boats, and the flowers no name — they are 'fleurs de rêve',

magic flowers. This primitive world is on the edge of a sea, and
there is a reference to a flood, precious stones, and rainbows;
but these echoes of 'Après le déluge' only serve to emphasise
fundamental differences between the two poems. The sea, which
before was static as in an engraving, is now an active particip-
ant; the Flood, instead of destroying, has become a 'clair déluge',
a spring of life rising from the meadows; the precious stones no
longer bury themselves, but stand erect; the 'chaos de glaces'
has disappeared and all has thawed as the new order brings
warmth and freedom. Instead of a single rainbow, there are
many, and they combine with the flowers and the sea to cele-
brate the birth of a purified world. In contrast to 'Après le déluge', where the occupations and activities of human beings,
as of animals and things, were unrelated to one another, in the
barbaric, richly coloured world of 'Enfance', people and objects
are linked by the same vital force to form a harmonious and
completely satisfying aesthetic pattern.

The third section deserves special attention if only because
it is a touchstone of our appreciation of Rimbaud's vision:

ENFANCE
III

Au bois il y a un oiseau, son chant vous arrête et vous fait
rougir.

Il y a une horloge qui ne sonne pas.

Il y a une fondrière avec un nid de bêtes blanches.

Il y a une cathédrale qui descend et un lac qui monte.

Il y a une petite voiture abandonnée dans le taillis, ou qui
descend le sentier en courant, enrubannée.

Il y a une troupe de petits comédiens en costumes, aper-
çus sur la route à travers la lisière du bois.

Il y a enfin, quand l'on a faim et soif, quelqu'un qui
vous chasse.

Because this 'Il y a' poem is itself both simple and complex, clear
and ambiguous, it has given rise to numerous interpretations
ranging from the naive to the overcomplicated. In his book,
Le Symbolisme, André Barre sees in it nothing but extreme simplicity and artlessness;[9] Michel Deguy on the other hand dis-
covers what he terms a 'pensée chercheuse', a thought that

searches and, in searching, calls in question the nature not only of language but of the world itself.[10] Between the two extremes is the matter-of-fact viewpoint of those who believe that there exist in history or in the life of the poet incidents or facts which *explain* the poem. Thus, M. Jacques Gengoux sees in the seven sentences of 'Il y a' seven symbols of the childhood of humanity during the Middle Ages,[11] while M. Antoine Adam believes that the poem is about Rimbaud's own childhood.[12] Professor Alan Chisholm shares this view and states categorically: 'The *Enfance* context makes it certain that these are reminiscences of childhood and "vous" refers to the poet as a small boy, as it does also in "Au bois il y a un oiseau, son chant *vous* arrête et *vous* fait rougir"'; and he adds that we can imagine Rimbaud as a boy walking in the country round Charleville, '(not alone, alas)' because 'there is always *quelqu'un* to hustle him along'.[13] But even if the context is childhood, it is an exceptional one – a childhood 'après le déluge'.

Nothing could be simpler than the expression 'il y a'. Today it is used as a featureless pointer or worn-out sign, but in this text, where the language is as young as the experience, it is endowed with full verbal force, and several possible functions. Does, for example, this particular 'il y a' evoke a real past time of which only the memory remains, or is it the fairy-tale 'il y avait une fois' suddenly become present reality? Or does it suggest something that may exist somewhere in the future? Or something that could never exist and can only be imagined? Or is its function to introduce and situate images in a fugitive yet eternal present – the time of the reading of the poem? Or is it a *simultanéiste* picture (as later in Apollinaire's 'Il y a' poems), which brings together different events that are taking place at one and the same time to form a verbal collage?

This ambiguity, that is to say richness of suggestion and meaning, characterises the poem, where one hears, as in 'Voyelles', two voices. The first is like that of a child relating a story or reading a lesson, as Rimbaud's schoolboy friend Ernest Delahaye perceived when he described the poem as 'une historiette en un style enfantin'. The other voice is that of the *voyant*, announcing an experiment, the experiment of seeing, and of making us see. The manner of seeing also links child and *voyant*. The child's way is to see things one after the other de-

tached from their context, 'un oiseau', 'une horloge', 'une fondrière', 'un nid', 'une cathédrale', 'un lac', etc.; but the *voyant*
has the power to distinguish the singular among the plurality
and to give it unique power. 'Enfance' combines the child-like
vision with an elementary exercise in *voyance*. After the brutal
but salutary shock of 'Après le déluge', Rimbaud seeks to awaken
and exercise our minds, to make us change our habitual way
of seeing so that we see, and hear, as it were, for the first time.
He offers us, as he says in 'Solde', 'l'occasion, unique, de dégager
nos sens!' Even in the least surprising sentences — the third,
fifth, sixth and seventh — there is a sense of strangeness and
mystery. What are the white creatures in a nest? Why is the little
carriage abandoned, and why does it start to run down the
path? Who are the little actors? Who are the 'someone' and the
'you' of the last sentence?

It is the first, second and fourth sentences, however, which
have most exercised the minds of readers. 'Au bois il y a un
oiseau, son chant vous arrête et vous fait rougir' surprises us
because usually we continue to walk and listen at the same time,
or we stop so that we can listen; but here it is the song of a bird
that makes us stop. In Apollinaire's poem 'L'Oiseau chante',
the song of a bird 'charms' the poet's ear, but it does not make
him stop or blush. And is 'rougir' to be interpreted as a flush of
pleasure, or of shame? Is the keenness of our joy mixed with
guilt because, preoccupied with everyday concerns, we have
never listened with undivided attention to anything as simple
and pure as *the* song of *a* bird?

The clock 'qui ne sonne pas' may be nature's clock, the sun;
or it may be a literary allusion, a silent reproach to the all-too-
talkative clock of Baudelaire's poem, 'L'Horloge'; or it may be a
symbol of the tyranny of time in our civilisation. But there is no
need to depart from the poem itself, where silence is as surprising as a song, and the absence of sound is as powerful as its
presence. In 'Enfance' we are in a world where eternity has
been rediscovered, a child embraces the summer dawn, and
clock-time no longer exists.

In the fourth sentence the statement is so paradoxical and
abnormal that it too has challenged the ingenuity of commentators. M. Jacques Gengoux interprets the cathedral which 'descends' as a symbol of the decadence and fall of the church,

while other critics see in it the Romantic image of trees in a wood rising like columns. But could it be that Rimbaud is simply describing something he saw as a child, a cathedral reflected in water; or something he saw in his imagination; or something he wanted to see happen, the normal world turned upside down? And is it, after all, so surprising to have — in a poem — a cathedral which 'descends'? We are conditioned by language which says that buildings 'go up', 'rise up', and that is how we normally look at them, from the bottom to the top. That is how Hugo, for example, saw and described the façade of the cathedral of Notre-Dame, first the doors, then the rose window, then the gallery, and finally the towers — an ascending movement of aspiration and prayer, the Romantic way of looking from earth to sky. But Rimbaud does not wish us to admire, as Hugo does, 'la tranquille grandeur de l'ensemble'; he invites us to reverse our way of seeing, so that the most stable objects and institutions 'descend'. To us, this visual exercise may seem pointless, but for Rimbaud it is a revolutionary gesture. His technique is similar in 'Mystique', where he reverses the conventional idea of a mystical aspiration towards heaven, and in a slow descending movement brings heaven down to us as a vision expressed in non-religious, purely human images.

In the last line of 'Enfance', most critics have taken the 'vous' to be the poet himself, in Albert Py's words 'enfant abandonné et menacé, repoussé'.[14] Albert Henry is of a similar opinion, that the meaning is 'Même au bois, il y a encore quelqu'un qui me chasse quand j'ai faim.'[15] The 'quelqu'un' may, however, be the poet and the 'vous' us, the readers, whom he drives away so that we cannot satisfy our hunger and thirst for 'reality'. Whatever interpretation is accepted, it would be misleading to stress the autobiographical nature of this poem. There is no explicit personal feeling, and the last line, like the others, is an incisive statement, unsentimental and objective. What is remarkable is the absence of nostalgia and of any reference to a 'je'.

In the fourth and fifth sections of 'Enfance', however, the 'je' is emphatically present. In the former, each of the first four sentences begins with a personal affirmation, as the poet announces several of the roles he plays here, as elsewhere in the *Illuminations*: 'Je suis le saint ... Je suis le savant ... Je suis le piéton ... Je serais bien l'enfant abandonné ... le petit valet ...', and, in section V, 'Je suis maître du silence . . .'. Some of these roles are those of the *voyant*, others those of the child. But Rimbaud, in his role of *voyant*, is not concerned with anything as personal or as limited as his own childhood, but with the childhood of a new world, and with the purity and the eternal 'jeunesse' of a primaeval force, life itself.

This much wider and fundamental conception is illustrated in 'Fleurs', a gem-like poem of only three sentences.

FLEURS

D'un gradin d'or, – parmi les cordons de soie, les gazes grises, les velours verts et les disques de cristal qui noircissent comme du bronze au soleil, –je vois la digitale s'ouvrir sur un tapis de filigranes d'argent, d'yeux et de chevelures.

Des pièces d'or jaune semées sur l'agate, des piliers d'acajou supportant un dôme d'émeraudes, des bouquets de satin blanc et de fines verges de rubis entourent la rose d'eau.

Tels qu'un dieu aux énormes yeux bleus et aux formes de neige, la mer et le ciel attirent aux terrasses de marbre la foule des jeunes et fortes roses.

How different in form and content this 'illumination' is from Hugo's 'contemplation', 'J'ai cueilli cette fleur pour toi sur la colline', where the flower is a flower, and its origin, destination, and the theme of the whole poem, are announced in the first line. And how original 'Fleurs' is compared with the Parnassian flora of lilies, lilacs, violets and roses, which Rimbaud had satirised in 'Ce qu'on dit au poète à propos de fleurs'. In spurning those conventional flowers, he urged the Parnassian leader, Théodore de Banville (to whom the poem was addressed), to be both more inventive and more practical, and to find useful flowers which would blossom into scarlet trousers for the French army, or 'des Fleurs qui soient des chaises'. Rimbaud himself does not follow this amusing advice, and his flowers here are useless, as are the 'fleurs de rêve' of 'Enfance', 'qui tintent, éclatent, éclairent'. They are the new flowers to which he refers in *Une Saison en enfer*: 'J'ai essayé d'inventer de nouvelles fleurs . . .'.

Enid Starkie, who tended to overstress the importance of

alchemy, as others have of drugs, in Rimbaud's poetry, saw in
'Fleurs' imagery borrowed from books of magic and alchemy,
the term 'flower' being, for the alchemists, 'the pure substance
in the metal, the spirit of matter'.[16] One could just as well say
that the imagery was taken from books on botany and garden-
ing: reading 'cordon', for example, as a grassy border, or a stalk
joining the seed to the placenta; 'velours' as smooth lawns;
'disque' as the centre of certain flowers; 'tapis' as used in the
expressions 'tapis de verdure' and 'tapis de gazon', meaning
greensward. 'Chevelure' could be the feathery 'tail' of a seed;
'satin blanc' is a name for the plant honesty; and 'verge' is
found in 'verge d'or', golden rod. But the main point is not where
the words came from, but how they are organised as a poem,
and the powers of suggestion they have acquired through Rimbaud's imagination and technique. The alchemy is now in the
words themselves. And does it really matter if 'rose d'eau' is
not to be found in any book? There are 'rose de diamants', 'rose
des sables', 'rose de ciel', 'rose des vents', so why not this humble
and unique 'rose d'eau'?

The 'rose d'eau' is the calm companion of the flower in
'Mémoire', the 'souci d'eau', a marsh marigold, but also a symbolic flower. In 'Fleurs' the 'rose d'eau' is the poem's still centre,
surrounded by a wealth of sensuous imagery — poetic flora —
and colours. It is also the centre of a gradation of colours from
the foxglove, to the rubies, to the roses. Motionless, it lies between two movements: the opening of the foxgloves, and the
roses being drawn up to the marble terraces. It is a moment of
repose and contemplation before the eye, having descended with
the poet's gaze from the 'gradin d'or' to the 'tapis' ('un tapis . . .
d'yeux'), moves up to the eyes of the god-like figure at the end.
The importance of the last sentence is emphasised by the more
marked use of assonance and internal rhymes ('dieu', 'yeux',
'bleu', 'énormes', 'formes'), and by the stresses in a rhythm
ascending to the profusion of roses which symbolise the fecundity and vitality of all that exists in Rimbaud's new world.

'Fleurs', which was for Ernest Delahaye 'une fête de couleurs',
and for Albert Thibaudet 'tout en lumière', is more than an
original poem about flowers. It is an illuminating evocation of
the 'future Vigueur' which Rimbaud had sought in 'Le Bateau
ivre', and of the principle of growth itself, first in the one ('la

digitale'), then in the many ('la foule des jeunes et fortes roses').
This sense of fecundity is conveyed not only at the end, but
throughout the poem, by the clusters of concrete nouns in the
plural, and by verbs in the present tense which, in each of the
sentences, make us feel that we are actually sharing, as in 'Enfance', the wonder of Rimbaud's vision. The impression of sharing in a special way of looking — and of looking at something
unique — is emphasised by the nature of the viewpoint. The
reader, as in other *Illuminations*, becomes a spectator in an imaginary theatre; and here, he is made to look down, 'd'un gradin
d'or', with all his attention focused, on to a stage which is at
once minute and infinite.

The town, like childhood, is one of the major themes in the
Illuminations. It is a theme which spans the whole of Rimbaud's
work from the 'Prologue', in which he had dreamed about being
born in the town of Rheims, to the 'Adieu' of *Une Saison en enfer*,
where he prepares to enter the 'splendides villes'; but it is in the
Illuminations that it is given supreme artistic expression. Rimbaud is both fascinated and repelled by the size and the novelty
of the modern city, by what Baudelaire called the vast 'paysages
de pierre', and he finds in its splendours, as in its monstrosities,
a fresh source of inspiration. At the same time, he sees it as the
symbol of a materialistic civilisation, and an obstacle to his
desire to live, 'étincelle d'or de la lumière *nature*', in union with
nature's elemental forces.
   Six of the prose poems — 'Ouvriers', 'Les Ponts', 'Ville',
'Villes I' ('Ce sont des villes!...'), 'Villes II' ('L'acropole offi-
cielle...') and 'Métropolitain' —are given entirely to this theme,
and in most of the others the town is either mentioned or suggested. In 'Enfance', a 'ville monstrueuse', with its houses,
sewers, fog and endless night, exists side by side with azure
chasms, wells of fire, moons, comets, seas and fables; and in
'Promontoire' an extraordinary variety of natural and man-
made features from different towns, countries and continents
are ingeniously interwoven into an immense fantasy of palace,
city and promontory that takes the mind into a realm of limitless space and potentiality.
   It would be difficult to find in any other small group of poems
such variety and such differences. 'Villes I' and 'Villes II', for

instance, are totally opposed. The former is made up of elements from past ages — primitive, heroic, classical, and so on — integrated into a vision of a world cleansed by nature's revitalised forces and man's immemorial ideals of love and fraternity. It is a festival of living together in harmonious activity without modern towns and with none of the 'machinery' of life. 'Villes II', in contrast, is essentially modern, even sinister, in atmosphere and feeling; and the pervasive sense of estrangement, the overwhelming architecture, the incomprehensible laws, and the 'drames assez sombres' seem to announce the age of Kafka and Michaux, and the hideous sprawl of twentieth-century megalopolis.

Each of these poems consists of a plurality of towns and cities, the known fused with the imagined, the real with the visionary. Actual places are mentioned — the Alleghenies, Lebanon, Bagdad, Hampton Court, the Sainte-Chapelle, London, Paris; but these and other familiar features are transformed by a rigorously controlled modification of viewpoints, perspectives and lighting — pictorial devices which Rimbaud uses, not as Verlaine does to make a scene imprecise and impressionistic, but to give clarity and definition. The constant element which unites these singularly diverse poems is technique, for they are the result, directly or indirectly, of Rimbaud's 'long, immense et raisonné *dérèglement* de *tous les sens*'. They are also illuminating insights into aspects of the industrial age, from its potential beauty to its sordid mediocrity and anonymity.

Rimbaud is both the spectator and the inhabitant of the imaginary towns he has constructed, but he usually writes from the viewpoint of an ecstatic, and at times bewildered, observer, contemplating the town from the outside. 'Ville' is, however, an exception. Although in various ways he marks his detachment from this town and its citizens ('l'*extérieur* des maisons', '*ces* millions des gens', '*de* ma fenêtre', '*devant* mon cottage') he also seems to place himself within it: 'Je suis un éphémère et point trop mécontent citoyen d'une métropole crue moderne . . .'. In the view of some critics, this metropolis is London, where Rimbaud lived on three occasions between 1872 and 1874, a hypothesis which is supported by the opposition between 'ces millions de gens' and 'les peuples du continent', the use of the

English word 'cottage', and the reference to the 'épaisse et éternelle fumée de charbon'.[17] This town, however, is neither 'la Ville' nor 'une Ville', but 'Ville': both particular and general, the nature and essence of every town and city, the 'idea' of a town. Similarly, the 'je' is at once the narrator, Rimbaud, and Everyman. 'Ville' may be a satire on London and its inhabitants, but it is more than that. It is a statement about the condition of man in an urban environment.

VILLE

Je suis un éphémère et point trop mécontent citoyen d'une métropole crue moderne parce que tout goût connu a été éludé dans les ameublements et l'extérieur des maisons aussi bien que dans le plan de la ville. Ici vous ne signaleriez les traces d'aucun monument de superstition. La morale et la langue sont réduites à leur plus simple expression, enfin! Ces millions de gens qui n'ont pas besoin de se connaître amènent si pareillement l'éducation, le métier et la vieillesse, que ce cours de vie doit être plusieurs fois moins long que ce qu'une statistique folle trouve pour les peuples du continent. Aussi comme, de ma fenêtre, je vois des spectres nouveaux roulant à travers l'épaisse et éternelle fumée de charbon, — notre ombre des bois, notre nuit d'été! — des Érinnyes nouvelles, devant mon cottage qui est ma patrie et tout mon cœur puisque tout ici ressemble à ceci, — la Mort sans pleurs, notre active fille et servante, un Amour désespéré, et un joli Crime piaulant dans la boue de la rue.

Several words in the opening sentence, especially 'crue moderne' and 'éludé', suggest that the narrator is interested in the modern (cf. 'Il faut être absolument moderne' in *Une Saison en enfer*), but at the same time disillusioned with this particular kind of modernity. With point and irony 'éludé' not only explains 'crue moderne', but implies that man has successfully used his ingenuity to eliminate any appearance of taste from all aspects of the town. In the same way, he has used his intelligence to reduce his inner life as well as his external life to a level that is impersonal, vulgar and statistical. In 'Ville', the inhabitants do not need to know one another because they all live the same standardised three-phase existence: education, a job, old age.

'Ces millions de gens' are millions of ciphers in a world governed by the logic of statistics, which has replaced religion as the 'monument de superstition'. As if to illustrate this 'logic', the words 'Aussi comme' of the final sentence introduce, not a clearly articulated statement, but one that is involved and syntactically obscure; yet like insistent beats, they announce with implacable logic the only 'vision' left to modern man. Its reality is stressed by the present tenses ('je vois . . . est . . . ressemble'); and by a series of words and expressions which situate the scene ('de ma fenêtre . . . devant mon cottage . . . ici . . . ceci . . . dans la boue de la rue'). The reader experiences the same sense of nearness and intimacy as in another and very different illumination, 'Mystique', where a beautiful image is seen 'contre notre face'. In 'Ville', however, we are confronted with ugliness, enduring horror and spiritual loss, conveyed by implicit references to a past heritage.

In the first sentence there is an allusion to the Bible and, as has been suggested by V. P. Underwood, Rimbaud may be recalling Saint Paul's declaration: 'I am a citizen of no mean city.'[18] In the last sentence, 'notre ombre des bois, notre nuit d'été' looks back to the Elizabethan age, to *A Midsummer Night's Dream* and, with 'les Érinnyes', to the Furies of Greek tragedy. The one mention of nature in 'Ville' — 'Notre ombre des bois, notre nuit d'été' — placed in apposition to 'l'épaisse et éternelle fumée de charbon', which has become the town-dweller's substitute for woodland shade and summer night, is a potent reminder of the extent to which man has laid waste and destroyed his heritage.

In the conclusion, where the street is full of echoes and spectres, the word 'cottage' strikes an odd note and seems at first reading as out of place as does the polar 'Splendide-Hôtel' in 'Après le déluge'. Each, however, is an expression of the bourgeois mentality: the 'Splendide-Hôtel' embodying grandiose ideas about travel abroad, and the 'cottage' illusions about 'home sweet home'. Moreover, 'cottage', like so many words in this text, links the present with the past, and one recalls, because of the preceding reference to Greek literature, the 'Ulysse' of Du Bellay's sonnet, for whom a 'pauvre maison' was 'une province et beaucoup davantage'. The fact that the 'cottage', for the narrator, is his 'patrie et tout [son] cœur' may also be a derisive allusion to the proverbial saying that an Englishman's home is his castle. The Erinnyes, put into modern dress and allegorised as three figures in a sinister urban ballet – pitiless Death, despairing Love and pretty Crime – no longer pursue man. They face him, the projection of his crimes and perverted desires; and even if these new Furies are seen only by the *voyant*, they are Everyman's punishment.

At the end of 'Ville' the vision is not suddenly destroyed, as it is in 'Les Ponts'; there is no nostalgic lament, as in 'Villes I'; and the poet does not express a wish to escape from the all-enveloping urban scene, as he does in 'Ouvriers'. 'Ville' is sharply focused and stable, and in it Rimbaud's power as a *voyant* has acquired a prophetic realism. The final image of Crime, reinforced by a lingering, abject whimper ('piaulant'), recalls the jackals 'piaulant' as they moved furtively through the 'déserts de thym' of 'Après le déluge'; but here Crime, ironically described as 'joli', flaunts itself openly in the deserts of the town. 'Ville' is Rimbaud's most lucid and terrifying illumination of man's plight and depravity in the industrial age.

In most editions of the *Illuminations*, 'Ville' is immediately followed by 'Ornières'; and the juxtaposition, even if fortuitous, is interesting. This poem is related more to those about childhood, such as 'Enfance' and 'Aube', than to the town poems; for here the presence of the town is only suggested ('parc' and 'suburbaine'). We have moved from darkness to light, from a drab adult environment to a brightly coloured, enchanted world. Moreover, the contrast between the two poems illustrates different meanings of the term 'illumination'. 'Ville' is an illumination in a spiritual sense, about 'progress' and the impoverishment of life; 'Ornières' is a coloured picture to which depth, movement and meaning are given. The title, a single word as with many of the *Illuminations*, could equally well be that of a still-life painting; but it has none of the slowness and immobility usually associated with ruts.

ORNIÈRES

À droite l'aube d'été éveille les feuilles et les vapeurs et les bruits de ce coin du parc, et les talus de gauche tiennent dans leur ombre violette les mille rapides ornières de la route humide. Défilé de féeries. En effet: des chars chargés d'animaux de bois doré, de mâts et de toiles bariolées, au grand galop de vingt chevaux de cirque tachetés, et les enfants et les hommes sur leurs bêtes les plus étonnantes; — vingt véhicules, bossés, pavoisés et fleuris comme des carrosses anciens ou de contes, pleins d'enfants attifés pour une pastorale suburbaine. — Même des cercueils sous leur dais de nuit dressant les panaches d'ébène, filant au trot des grandes juments bleues et noires.

The first sentence, which sets the scene, directs attention to the most important parts of the picture: 'À droite ... ce coin du parc ... les talus de gauche ...'. The slow but alert rhythm, and the taut vowel sounds 'e' and 'i', suggest the tension of awakening life, to which the 'ombre violette' gives depth as well as colour. Another effective juxtaposition, 'rapides' and 'ornières', a noun normally associated with ideas of routine and slowness, produces a pleasurable sensation of surprise, and frees us from habitual ways of thinking and seeing. The device also serves to animate the perspective, and to lead to the 'défilé' of the central section. The everyday adverbial expression 'en effet', like the 'il y a' in 'Enfance', is also revitalised and given a special force. It initiates an 'effect', or illusion, so vivid and convincing that the 'défilé de féeries' becomes a reality. Suddenly the picture is alive and the procession appears to move out of the frame and advance towards us. Despite the absence of verbs, an impression of movement 'au grand galop' is created by the simple device of naming things, animals and people, in quick succession; by an accelerating tempo; and by the repetition of sounds (alliteration and assonance) and words, notably 'de' and 'et'. A more subtle device is the placing of nearly all the adjectives after the nouns they qualify, which has the effect of pulling them along and investing them with motion. As well as an impression of size conveyed by the repetition of 'vingt', a physical sense of the clustering together of participants in the procession is achieved by the way in which words, carried along by the rhythms they create, press and crowd on each other. Words that are similar in meaning — for example, 'chars', 'véhicules', 'carrosses', and the sequence 'animaux', 'chevaux' and 'bêtes' — are also a functional part of this dynamic effect. At the end, the pace slackens from a 'grand galop' to a 'trot', and the rhythm becomes slower as befits the changed funereal context, in which sombre objects, 'cercueils', 'plumes d'ébène', 'dais de nuit', and the 'juments bleues et noires', contrast with the multicoloured part of the procession. In a poem where everything is closely related, the last sentence recalls by echoes and contrasts all that has preceded, and in particular the opening sentence. The colours in the 'ombre violette' of dawn and unfolding life have separated into the 'bleues' and 'noires' of night and death, and the two participles, especially 'filant', prolong the action indefinitely and give the ending and the whole poem special significance.

Ernest Delahaye believed that 'Ornières' was inspired by a travelling American circus which the poet had seen in the Place Ducale in Charleville; but even if this text is the memory of something seen, it has been transmuted by Rimbaud's imagination to become, as he himself says, a 'défilé de féeries'. 'Ornières' is more than a 'souvenir', and more than a picture. It is a symbol of human life, a miniature 'comédie humaine' with, at the beginning, dawn and awakening life; at the end, words, objects and colours associated with night and death; and in the middle, a motley cavalcade of children, people, animals and things, seized in a brief moment between day and night, birth and death.

The summer dawn, which in 'Ornières' awakes nature, is itself the subject of 'Aube'. A number of references to the dawn occur throughout Rimbaud's work. In 'Le Bateau ivre', dawn is 'un peuple de colombes'; in 'Bonne pensée du matin' (which, like 'Aube', ends on the word 'midi') the summer dawn inspires the poet's 'bonne pensée' for the workers; the 'aurores' give to the conclusion of 'Comédie de la soif' the same kind of purity and freshness that characterise 'Aube'; 'Promontoire', one of the *Illuminations*, begins with 'l'aube d'or', while in 'Adieu', the last section of *Une Saison en enfer*, dawn is invoked to mark both a conclusion and a fresh beginning. In 'Aube', the dawn, 'cette heure indicible, première du matin' (as Rimbaud wrote in a letter in June 1872 to Delahaye), is personified and presented with another character, the child-poet; and, as in 'Ornières', the theme of childhood and of life is presented (but in a form at once purer and more complex) against the background of the town:

AUBE

J'ai embrassé l'aube d'été.

Rien ne bougeait encore au front des palais.[19] L'eau était morte. Les camps d'ombres ne quittaient pas la route du bois. J'ai marché, réveillant les haleines vives et tièdes, et les pierreries regardèrent, et les ailes se levèrent sans bruit.

La première entreprise fut, dans le sentier déjà empli de frais et blêmes éclats, une fleur qui me dit son nom.

Je ris au wasserfall blond qui s'échevela à travers les sapins : à la cime argentée je reconnus la déesse.

Alors je levai un à un les voiles. Dans l'allée, en agitant les bras. Par la plaine, où je l'ai dénoncée au coq. À la grand' ville elle fuyait parmi les clochers et les dômes, et courant comme un mendiant sur les quais de marbre, je la chassais.

En haut de la route, près d'un bois de lauriers, je l'ai entourée avec ses voiles amassés, et j'ai senti un peu son immense corps. L'aube et l'enfant tombèrent au bas du bois.

Au réveil il était midi.

The poem begins with the last, but most important of a series of momentous events, and then reveals (as it were in flashback) how this event came about. The opening sentence announces an extraordinary fact in the most natural and simple language. It could stand by itself as a *poème-phrase*, for in eight syllables, rhythmically assonated by the four 'e' sounds, Rimbaud has condensed the joy and the triumph which are the essence of the poem. One is reminded of the lyric, 'L'Éternité': 'Elle est retrouvée/Quoi? – L'Éternité/C'est la mer allée/Avec le soleil', where Eternity is seen as something as natural as the union between the sea and the sun. In much the same way, the child and the dawn 'go together', and finally fall together.

The first section is composed of two almost equal parts, the first made up of three sentences, the second of a single sentence, and together they form a contrasted sequence in which inactivity is followed by movement. In the first half, Rimbaud evokes the silence and the mystery of a sleeping landscape with its palaces, stagnant water, and encamped shadows. The word

'palais' is unexpected, but this is an enchanted world in which
everything is transformed by the light of dawn and by the poet's
vision. 'Les camps d'ombres', an original image, suggests the
dormant vitality of the sleeping shadows (in contrast with the
'dead' water) which are ready to strike camp at the first light of
dawn, or rather, at the first movement of the poet. It is he, the
animator and life-giver, who awakens (or imagines that he
awakens) the landscape. This awakening, as hushed and as
strange as the previous immobility, is conveyed in the second
part of the section by a quickening tempo; by a change from
imperfect tenses of description to past tenses of action; and by the
thrice repeated 'et', the last two being used, as in the biblical
manner, to give authority to the statement. In this long sentence
each word is at once definite and rich with suggestions. 'Haleines' may refer to something as precise as the breathing of
animals, or the early mists and breezes; 'pierreries' may be
stones seen as precious stones (just as houses are seen as palaces),
or stones covered with gleaming dew, or the dew sparkling in
the light; 'ailes' may be the birds, or the darkness, silently taking flight. But the total impression, produced in part by the use
of plural nouns and adjectives, is that of the actual presence, the
warmth, and the vibrant potentiality of awakening life.

In the next sentence, the first words, 'La première entreprise . . .',
strike a grave yet naively heroic note as they announce a momentous event. Wonder and expectation are further heightened by
variations in the rhythm; and by penetration into the wood,
from the 'route' to a 'sentier', where we see — and feel — the
first cool gleams of light (there is a difference of temperature
between the 'haleines' that are 'vives et tièdes' and the 'éclats de
lumière' that are 'frais et blêmes'). In this setting, a flower declares its name. Coming after so many words in the plural, 'une
fleur', unaccompanied by any qualifying adjective, stands out
with sharp clarity. This example of animism is reminiscent of
other examples in the work of Nerval, Hugo, and Baudelaire;
but Rimbaud's flower that speaks is unique in its utter naturalness. This climax is so simple as to be almost an anti-climax;
but the apparent spontaneity is the revelation of a power (as
godlike as the power to create by naming) that compels nature
to reveal her secrets. The realisation of this power produces the
ecstasy which, in the following section, is expressed by laughter.

The poet's laughter at the waterfall, a force that corresponds to his own exultant energy, is not an expression of harmony with nature in the Romantic manner, but rather pagan delight, pride, and even defiance. The rest of this section describes two contrary movements: the water falling, and the poet looking up. The sudden reversal of direction from 'à travers les sapins' to 'à la cime argentée' emphasises the swiftness of the poet's perception of the 'déesse', and turns the moment of recognition into a *movement* of recognition. This is the real climax and it comes at the centre of the poem.

In a series of sensitively varied and increasingly vital rhythms, the poem has progressed to this central point, from a shadowy expanse to flashes of bright colour, from 'dead' water to living water and a source of life — the dawn goddess. The personification may seem conventional, by contrast with that of the 'wasserfall',[20] where the adjective 'blond' and the verb 's'échevela' convey in a visual and dynamic image the impression of sunlight on water, tumbling between rocks and boulders. But the personification of the dawn as a goddess (or the Muse of poetry), precisely because it relates 'Aube' to innumerable other dawns in literature, throws into high relief Rimbaud's skill in transforming a conventional 'figure' into a presence and a force.

From a momentarily static point, the poem opens out; and from 'Alors' to 'je la chassais' all is excited movement, first staccato, then continuous. Pursuit and flight are conveyed by nouns — 'l'allée', 'la plaine', 'la grand'ville' — which widen the perspective from the countryside to the town; and more explicitly by a series of verbs, the changes in tense and form suggesting the vicissitudes and the breathless continuity of the chase. But first there are three short sentences in which the poet seeks to unveil the mystery. The child waving his arms recalls the child in 'Après le déluge' ('l'enfant tourna ses bras, compris des girouettes et des coqs des clochers de partout')' but whereas, in that first 'illumination', he was understood by the weather-vanes and the steeple-cocks because his action resembled theirs, in 'Aube' he usurps the cock's function. It is he who announces to that usually vigilant herald of the dawn the presence of the goddess. But 'dénoncée', as well as having the sense of 'announced', may also mean 'denounced' because, in the child-poet's

view, the dawn's flight implies treachery and guilt. The dura-
tion of the flight is effectively suggested in the next sentence
by its length; by the present participle 'courant' (prolonged by
the assonance of 'mendiant'); by the use of an imperfect tense
('fuyait') at the beginning, and another ('chassais') at the end,
the last of these having the effect of immeasurably extending the
movement and of carrying it over into the next section. The
inversion of the previous order so that the goddess — 'elle' — is
now placed at the beginning of the sentence, and the 'je' at the
end, does more than introduce a change into the structure; it
stresses the poet's inferior role as pursuer and suppliant. Far
above him the dawn continues to light up the highest points,
the 'clochers' and the 'dômes'; while he, now described as a
beggar, runs along the 'quais de marbre'. His state as a 'mendiant' is underlined by contrast with the richness suggested by
the 'marbre', itself an ironic echo of the 'palais' at the beginning
of the poem.

A slower rhythm marks the penultimate section, which describes the end and the result of this 'chasse spirituelle'. We have
moved from the 'quais de marbre' to 'en haut de la route'; where
the laurels, which recall the tradition of the crowning of a vic-
torious poet with a laurel wreath, and the legend of Apollo's
unsuccessful pursuit of Daphne, stand as an ambiguous symbol
of victory. The dawn, enveloped again in her veils, does not
reveal her secret; and the child, although he embraces the
goddess, only touches a fraction of her immense body. Together
they fall at the edge of the wood. At the dénouement, the 'je'
is generalised as 'l'enfant'; and the poem is given a universal
application. Then time breaks into the timeless world of childhood: 'Au réveil il était midi.' The last line is as taut as the first,
and its eight syllables re-echo the eight syllables of the opening
line. But the tense 'i' sounds introduce a different note, and with
the pause coming after the third instead of the fourth syllable,
this line, unlike the first, is neither symmetrical nor perfectly
balanced. These slight formal differences may indicate a certain disenchantment, but if there is disenchantment there is no
self-pity in the final statement. Moreover, the first line, and not
the last, may be intended to express the essence of 'Aube': rap-
ture at having seen the beauty, and touched, if only 'un peu' and
for a moment, the body of the dawn. Together, the brief open-

ing and concluding lines express, in a 'visual lyricism', the enigma of the poem. They are like the arms of the child ('Oh! bras trop courts!' as Rimbaud exclaims at the end of 'Mémoire') which, while embracing, are unable to hold the dawn.

This poem of impressions, sensations, movement, and of awakening and developing vitality, has several possible meanings (and there seems no reason to follow modern practice and put the last word in inverted commas). 'Aube' expresses the desire for a special kind of union with nature, and in it Rimbaud achieves one of his frequently stated aims, to live 'étincelle d'or de la lumière *nature*'. It also expresses his search for the 'future Vigueur', the new kind of inspiration he mentions in 'Le Bateau ivre'; and for the new visions, which were the aim of the *voyant*. In a more general sense, 'Aube' is an aspiration towards purity and the ideal, unhindered and uncomplicated by remorse, Romantic ennui or Baudelairian spleen. On the human plane, 'Aube' is the journey from childhood to 'maturity'; from the brief period when the child is a poet, creator and bearer of life; when things are always seen and felt 'for the first time'; and visions are a present reality, but abruptly disappear when we reach the midday of life. 'Aube', with its two main characters, the child and the dawn goddess, also represents and plays out Rimbaud's (and the child's) conflict with the mother, a struggle in which the 'coq' (symbol of the awakening of desire as well as of life) is an accomplice. The child and the dawn may also represent conflicting parts of Rimbaud's own nature, and in this respect 'Aube' is related to other *Illuminations*, such as 'Conte' and 'Royauté', where a momentary synthesis, or union, is likewise achieved. It is not only a 'coloured plate', a remarkably luminous picture, but also an 'illumination' in a deeper sense: one of the rare moments when the *voyant* sees; and experiences an intense, if ephemeral, ecstasy.

With delicacy and power, concretely, sensuously, and with a pure immediacy, Rimbaud has not only expressed in 'Aube' the beauty, the immaculate freshness, and the very feel of the dawn; he has also expressed in symbolic form his search for the completeness and fulfilment that he constantly sought, but was never able to achieve, except imaginatively, in creative moments of illumination, one of which is 'Aube'.

With 'Barbare' we are taken beyond time, people, countries
and towns — outside our world — to witness the barbaric dawn
of a new form of life:

BARBARE

Bien après les jours et les saisons, et les êtres et les pays,
Le pavillon en viande saignante sur la soie des mers et des
fleurs arctiques; (elles n'existent pas.)
Remis des vieilles fanfares d'héroïsme — qui nous atta-
quent encore le cœur et la tête — loin des anciens assassins —
Oh! Le pavillon en viande saignante sur la soie des mers
et des fleurs arctiques; (elles n'existent pas.)
Douceurs!
Les brasiers, pleuvant aux rafales de givre, — Douceurs! —
les feux à la pluie du vent de diamants jetée par le cœur
terrestre éternellement carbonisé pour nous.
— Ô monde! —
(Loin des vieilles retraites et des vieilles flammes, qu'on
entend, qu'on sent,)
Les brasiers et les écumes. La musique, virement des
gouffres et choc des glaçons aux astres.
Ô Douceurs, ô monde, ô musique! Et là, les formes, les
sueurs, les chevelures et les yeux, flottant. Et les larmes
blanches, bouillantes, — ô douceurs! — et la voix féminine
arrivée au fond des volcans et des grottes arctiques.
Le pavillon...

The opening line and the reference to 'vieilles flammes' have
been used to show that this is one of the *Illuminations* written
after *Une Saison en enfer*, that is, after 1873; and supporting evidence has been found in certain expressions which, it is thought,
Rimbaud may have taken from Flaubert's *La Tentation de Saint-
Antoine*, first published in 1874. Other details have suggested
that 'Barbare' may have been written as late as 1877, when Rimbaud is supposed to have made a journey to the North Pole;
and in this reductive reading the 'pavillon' becomes a Scandin-
avian flag, the 'brasiers' Icelandic geysers, and the 'musique'
the thunderous noise of the maelstrom heard near Lofoten. This
misuse of a text in the search for facts and chronological clues
is particularly perverse in the case of 'Barbare' where the poet,
dispensing with all anecdotal and story aspects (still evident in
'Après le déluge'), endeavours to express what he had never

before seen or experienced, and to give form to the half-formed and the formless. But in spite of this detective work, it has so far proved impossible, as with other *Illuminations*, to assign a definite date to 'Barbare'; and the text itself remains ambiguous and enigmatic.

The 'pavillon en viande saignante' is perhaps the most discussed image in the whole of Rimbaud's work. What is the 'pavillon'? Is the 'viande saignante' bleeding meat, or a blood-red colour? The majority of commentators have taken it to be a colour and the 'pavillon' a flag — the Norwegian, blue cross on a red background; or Danish, white cross on a red background; or the French tricolour or the Union Jack, each of them red, white and blue. For others, it is a red flag of revolution, a banner of freedom and liberation, a symbolic flag — that of the *voyant* himself. Indeed, 'pavillon' as a flag does seem a probable meaning; and it relates to other flags in Rimbaud's poetry, the 'drapeaux d'extase' of 'Génie' and the 'pavillons multicolores' in the 'Adieu' of *Une Saison en enfer*. The 'pavillon' has also been seen as a small building, a shelter, tent or pavilion — the pavilion at the International Exhibition in London in 1872, with the 'viande saignante' the vast panels 'd'une brique sanguine et vivante', as Mallarmé described them; or a poetic, imaginary pavilion, more original than the 'pavillon de ténèbres tendues' in Baudelaire's 'La Chevelure'; or, at a deeper level, the symbol of the womb, the poem being an expression of a pre-natal experience. Other interpretations have been an abattoir, a volcano, and the sun, or more precisely the red conical-like rays of the setting sun, with Baudelaire again affording a relevant comparison, if not a source: 'Le soleil s'est noyé dans son sang qui se fige' ('Harmonie du soir').

More important than this conflict of interpretations are the intention and the theme of the poem. Is 'Barbare', as the title and the 'pavillon' image would indicate, a primitive, cruel and *barbaric* vision; or, because of the silk, the flowers, the 'douceurs' and the feminine voice, 'the most joyous and relaxed of all the *Illuminations*', as one commentator has put it?[21] One could state the problem in a more general way and ask whether birth or death is the main theme. Does 'Barbare' evoke the anguished birth of a new world; or, in a scene of Hiroshima-like destruction, the death throes of the old, reminding us of the conclusion of 'Soir historique', 'le moment de l'étuve, des mers enlevées, des embrasements souterrains, de la planète emportée, et des exterminations conséquentes ...'? Or is it, as is suggested by extremes that are held in a tensely poised equilibrium, the vision of a world at once barbaric and beautiful, for ever waiting to be born?[22] Rimbaud may have wished to exploit the aesthetic possibilities of ambiguous meanings and multiple interpretations. Whatever the correct or valid reading, he does not offer any explanation, but leaves words 'floating' and vulnerable, yet free to acquire or generate *other* meanings. As 'Barbare' is clearly a cosmic vision, like 'Après le déluge', 'Mystique', 'Soir historique' and 'Fleurs', it can reasonably be argued that 'pavillon' could have a less limiting meaning than 'flag' or 'pavilion' or even 'sun' and be taken as the canopy of the sky, the whole of nature, the world — as in Gilbert's famous 'Ode imitée de plusieurs psaumes', 'Ciel, pavillon de l'homme, admirable nature', a line which, significantly, is quoted, before 'pavillon' as a flag or banner, in a contemporary dictionary, *Nouveau dictionnaire classique de la langue française* (Bescherelle et Pons, 1868).

After an opening line which takes us beyond the human world of time, space and people, the 'pavillon en viande saignante' comes as a sharp and brutal shock. The nature of this image is, however, modified by the changing contexts; and its impact is both increased and diminished by 'la soie des mers', a visual-tactile image conveying the texture and feel of water, and by the 'fleurs arctiques', white foam on waves, or imaginary flowers, like the 'fleurs de rêve' of 'Enfance'. The tensions that result from the juxtaposition of different qualities and opposed sensations — enhanced by the colour contrast of red and white — exist in another form in the next line, where tension is generated by the conflict between past and present, between old destructive forces and a new creative power. When the 'pavillon' image occurs the second time, preceded by an 'Oh!', which may be of pleasure or of dread, it leads away from the false heroics of war and death (the 'vieilles fanfares' and the 'anciens assassins') to the fresh joys of 'Douceurs!', an exclamation which may be tinged with irony. But while the brutality of the image is toned down, its meaning in this ambiguous context becomes more mysterious and elusive.

Contrasts of fire and water, heat and cold, red and white are again linked in the next two lines, with the second extending the first upwards, and then downwards to lead to the 'cœur terrestre', the source of all these transformations of fire, water, air and earth. The 'cœur terrestre', which burns for us, is a secular transposition of the religious imagery of the flaming heart. Experiences from the past recur and invade the present, but although they can still be heard and felt they no longer attack. 'Loin' and the repeated 'vieilles' suggest that they have become more distant, or rather that the poet is moving away from them, and this impression is reinforced by the 'fading' effect produced by their being set in parenthesis. In the next line, 'écumes', the most abstract of the water images, is an appropriate transition and contrast to music, and to the auditory image, 'Virement des gouffres et choc des glaçons aux astres', which evokes, not the conventional music of the heavenly spheres, but the convulsive aspirations of primaeval forces.

'Ô Douceurs, ô monde, ô musique!' are unifying notes that have been sounded before. 'Douceurs' is heard four times in all, and is the dominant among these notes, whose function, in this essentially musical piece, is to harmonise extreme and disparate elements. The bringing together of these three nouns suggests that the conclusion will be a summing up and a coherent pattern or vision. But before this is reached, the opposite effect is produced, and our attention is suddenly directed to human phenomena and parts of the human body that are dispersed and 'floating': 'Et là, les formes, les sueurs, les chevelures et les yeux, flottant. Et les larmes blanches, bouillantes'. The tears remind us of 'le sel des larmes d'enfance' in 'Mémoire', and more especially of the sea, an 'éternité de chaudes larmes', in 'Enfance'; but here the tears, in keeping with the 'feux', 'brasiers' and 'volcans', are 'bouillantes'; for this is the childhood, or rather the birth-pangs, of a new world.

'Ô douceurs!' recurs at a key point of the conclusion and leads to a haunting promise of life in 'la voix féminine' (music made articulate); to the sense of achievement contained in 'arrivée'; and to the final synthesis of red and white, fire and water. The original image appears for the last time, reduced to its simplest, elemental form, 'Le pavillon . . .' — a *world* in travail; and a *word*, echoing back to the beginning of a poem which, in closing, it leaves suspended and open . . .[23]

The creative force, which is implicit and pervasive in the *Illuminations*, itself becomes a theme in a series of poems. It is usually embodied in imaginary figures and given the form of a parable or spiritual fable, as in 'Aube' and 'Conte'; but occasionally Rimbaud speaks in the first person, as in 'Phrases':

> J'ai tendu des cordes de clocher à clocher; des guirlandes de fenêtre à fenêtre; des chaînes d'or d'étoile à étoile, et je danse.

In this sentence, concrete nouns are stretched in a taut sequence consisting of two gradations which move rhythmically, as in a ballet, to the ecstatic climax, 'je danse'. The first is a process of transformation in which things become more precious and 'poetic' — from 'cordes' to 'guirlandes' to 'chaînes d'or'. The second is a dynamic upward movement to space and light — from 'clocher' to 'fenêtre' to 'étoile'. Without explanation or comment, Rimbaud has demonstrated his creative power; with one gesture he has transformed poetic space and our view of the world. This moment of lyrical joy, expressed in a single sentence, is one of the first and purest examples of the *poème-phrase* which has become, particularly since its cultivation by the Surrealists, a minor poetic genre.

But Rimbaud's poetic creed demands more than gestures, however effective and beautiful. To transform what is already there is not enough. The *voyant* must find words for what does not exist, or what has never yet been seen. In 'Matinée d'ivresse', which has all too often been regarded merely as one of the poems produced under the influence of hashish, Rimbaud reaffirms, with a certain irony, his faith in the *voyant*'s poetic method and the objects of his quest: a new and purer love, goodness and beauty. Despite his total dedication to a creed which is a torturing 'poison', the only results that he has achieved are announced in emphatic statements of a private nature, 'Ô *mon* Bien! Ô *mon* Beau!', and exclamations about the wonders of the unknown, 'Hourra pour l'œuvre inouïe et pour le corps merveilleux, pour la première fois!' By its very nature, the quest for perfection, the quintessential, the non-existent, must remain a quest, a permanent 'chasse spirituelle', in which the poet constantly appeals to what he alone can imagine. Consequently, in most of the poems about the new creative spirit,

Rimbaud is forced to use a special kind of rhetoric, at once incantatory and invocatory. Its aims are to ward off and counter influences from the material world and to produce a mood of exaltation. His art of persuasion is not concerned to convince us of the existence or importance of something real; but to persuade himself and the reader that the non-existent does exist and to create the illusion of its actual presence.

One of the finest examples of this is 'Génie', where the vision of a new Genius, or creative spirit, is fully developed and convincingly presented. In a continually modulating and flawless rhetorical sweep, Rimbaud brings together the facets that have occurred separately in other *Illuminations*, such as 'Vies', 'Angoisse', 'Solde' (the obverse and cynical counterpart of 'Génie'), 'Jeunesse' ('Sonnet'), and, in particular, 'À une raison'. 'Génie' is a hymn of praise to the revolutionary spirit of the poet himself, to his own genius, and also to a figure presented objectively as 'Il', the 'Génie', who is superior in love, compassion and power to God. The contrast between the 'Génie' and God is ironically emphasised by the use of religious ideas and terms in a non-religious way, and by *versets* and a rhetoric reminiscent of the Bible. In this poem, the rhetoric, which combines vast abstractions with precise images, is varied enough to convey (with a conviction that never falters) firstly, the actual existence of the 'Génie':

> Il est l'affection et le présent puisqu'il a fait la maison ouverte à l'hiver écumeux et à la rumeur de l'été, lui qui a purifié les boissons et les aliments, lui qui est le charme des lieux fuyants et le délice surhumain des stations. Il est l'affection et l'avenir, la force et l'amour que nous, debout dans les rages et les ennuis, nous voyons passer dans le ciel de tempête et les drapeaux d'extase.

Secondly, the multiplicity and the perfection of his qualities:

> Ô ses souffles, ses têtes, ses courses; la terrible célérité de la perfection des formes et de l'action.
> Ô fécondité de l'esprit et immensité de l'univers!

And thirdly, the dynamic force of his spirit which is active in every corner of the earth, linking all mankind:

> Il nous a connus tous et nous a tous aimés. Sachons, cette
> nuit d'hiver, de cap en cap, du pôle tumultueux au château,
> de la foule à la plage, de regards en regards, forces et sen-
> timents las, le héler et le voir, et le renvoyer, et sous les ma-
> rées et au haut des déserts de neige, suivre ses vues, ses
> souffles, son corps, son jour.

In the poems to the creative spirit, this accelerating movement and the widening of horizons at the end are unusual.
Most of them are a precarious balance of conflicting forces, and
when the rhetoric can no longer be sustained, and incantation
and invocation fail, echoes and images from the past intrude,
and there is a sudden return to the familiar world of reality.
This 'break' in inspiration occurs in many of the *Illuminations,*
but it is particularly significant in poems about poetry itself,
because it highlights the ambivalent nature of Rimbaud's genius;
its inherent limitations as well as its unusual power. At times,
as in 'Matinée d'ivresse' and 'Barbare', the poet seems to be a
passive spectator and his rhetoric powerless against hostile
forces which intrude at various points and threaten to destroy
the visionary world he has created. In other poems, he himself
becomes the destructive force; and in 'Aube' and 'Conte' it is he
who decides to end the 'comédie' and to bring down the curtain.
This underlines, in a brilliant shock-conclusion or enigmatic
postscript, the intrusion of reality, and what the poet feels to be
the inadequacy of his vision. But wherever these hostile forces
occur, and whatever their apparent nature, objective or subjective, their source is in Rimbaud himself. His daemon is both
creative and destructive; and the conflict between aims and
achievement is always present. Despite his overweening pride
in his own genius, he is at the same time conscious that, do what
he will with language, words are only words, what they reveal
is never absolutely new, and nothing is changed by them.

This double attitude is expressed in stark, almost brutal form
in 'Départ':

DÉPART

Assez vu. La vision s'est rencontrée à tous les airs.
Assez eu. Rumeurs des villes, le soir, et au soleil, et toujours.

Assez connu. Les arrêts de la vie. — Ô Rumeurs et Visions!
Départ dans l'affection et le bruit neufs!

The three statements 'Assez vu ... Assez eu ... Assez connu ...', while ostensibly rejecting past experience, suggest, by
their over-emphasis, its continuing and tenacious attraction. This
ambiguity is pervasive. The images are not precise, and the rhetoric does not define. Neither the old, which the poet rejects,
nor the new, which he seeks, is specified. The exclamatory 'Ô'
could express contempt or regret; and 'vision' and 'Visions'
are left vague and could be taken in a pejorative sense. But
even if the tension generated by the movement away from the
past and the thrust into the future remains unresolved, the stress
finally falls on 'départ' and 'neufs', the new climate of experience
which the poet is already in; and the total effect is optimistic
and exhilarating. There is no lassitude or ennui, as there is, for
example, in Mallarmé's 'Brise marine' where the departure is
towards an 'exotic nature'. 'Départ' is a clean break with the past
and a leap into the future; a rejection not only of what has become familiar and stale, but of a whole generation of literature
with its spleen and its *mal du siècle*. Rimbaud, as Jacques Rivière
said, 'vient nous empêcher de nous reconnaître au milieu des
objets familiers, d'y être à l'aise et contents; il vient ouvrir toutes
les fenêtres'.[24]

In his preface to the first edition of the *Illuminations*, Verlaine,
who was unable to discover in these texts any 'idée principale',
wrote enthusiastically about the 'prose exquise' and 'la plus
haute ambition (arrivée) de style'. Indeed, the originality of the
Illuminations does not lie in ideas, but in an unusual way of
looking at certain things, subjects and themes; and, as Verlaine
rightly stressed, in the style. In every phase of his literary career,
and in whatever medium — verse poem, free verse (of which he
was one of the inventors), prose poem or poetic prose — Rimbaud is both a revolutionary and a highly conscious craftsman;
but it is in the *Illuminations* that the originality of his experience
is matched by an unexampled sureness and intensity of expression.

His preoccupation with questions of form was already clear
in the *Lettre du voyant*, and there is some justification for his
arrogant comment on the 'meanness' of Baudelaire's style. He is

not as great a poet as Baudelaire, but he is more important as an innovator, above all in his imaginative use of the *poème en prose*. Faced with the same problem of how to give shape and coherence to a form of poetry which has abandoned the 'jeu ancien' of rhymes and stanzas, Rimbaud is the more inventive, and he comes nearer than Baudelaire to achieving the idea which the latter expressed in the preface to his own prose poems, *Le Spleen de Paris*: 'the miracle of a poetic prose, musical without rhythm or rhyme, supple and robust enough to express the lyrical movements of the soul, the undulations of dreams and the convulsions of the mind'. Baudelaire is generally regarded as the creator of the modern prose poem, and Rimbaud's debt to him is considerable. It is Rimbaud, however, who is the first to make the prose poem essentially poetic in content and form; and one of the obvious ways in which he does this is by the elimination of anecdotal material, of which there is still a great amount in the prose poems of Baudelaire. There is, it is true, a narrative element in 'Après le déluge' and in 'Conte'; but each of these ends with an enigmatic statement, and in neither is there any explanation or moral. Rimbaud also shortens the prose poem and makes it taut and compact by omitting prosaic elements, unnecessary words such as conjunctions, and certain inactive verbs. Instead of developing a theme through a logical sequence of sentences, he dislocates normal syntax and juxtaposes phrases, words and images. At times the only rule in his elliptical style appears to be the completely free association of words and ideas but, unlike the Surrealists who claim him as one of their illustrious predecessors, he never abandons himself passively to the dictates of the unconscious mind. His disordering of the senses is always reasoned and controlled.

To give the prose poem artistic form, Rimbaud uses several devices, including the refrain, and other kinds of repetition — of a sentence, an exclamation, a single word. In 'Barbare', 'Nocturne vulgaire' and 'H', for example, the first or second line is echoed in the last, though not exactly in the same way. In 'Barbare', 'Le pavillon en viande saignante sur la soie des mers et des fleurs arctiques; (elles n'existent pas.)', after occurring twice, preceded the second time by 'oh!', becomes at the end a truncated but potent refrain, 'Le pavillon . . .'. 'Nocturne vulgaire' begins 'Un souffle ouvre des brèches opéradiques . . . disperse

les limites des foyers' and ends with a change of emphasis as
'Un souffle disperse les limites du foyer.' The opening words of
'H', 'Toutes les monstruosités violent les gestes atroces d'Hortense' are echoed in the conclusion by the teasing challenge —
'trouvez Hortense'. In each case the effect is similar; the refrains
lead us back to the beginning and, as it were, encircle the poem
and bind it together. At the same time, the poem remains 'open'
as do most of the *Illuminations*, and so continues to engage and
enlarge the mind. In 'Matinée d'ivresse', alternating and opposed
refrains and repetitions are employed, and the two verbs 'com-
mencer' and 'finir', recurring at key points ('Cela commença . . .
cela finira . . . cela commença . . . cela finit . . . cela finit . . . cela
commençait . . . cela finit . . .'), give structural unity. They also
create a dialectical movement between past and future, which
is both resolved and held in suspense by the triumphant and
menacing affirmation: 'Voici le temps des *Assassins*.' The effect
of firmly 'closing' the poem, combined with the opposite effect
of keeping it 'open', is obtained by several other devices, such
as the question ('Enfance V', 'Villes I'); the oracular declaration
('Conte', 'Parade'); the shock-ending ('Matinée d'ivresse', 'Aube',
'Les Ponts'); and the explicit dynamic statement ('Départ',
'Génie'). In addition, assonance, alliteration and internal rhymes
also contribute to the inner vitality and coherence of the poem
by creating active links and a wide range of meanings.

Two examples of a particularly expressive — mimetic — relationship between form and content are 'Aube', and a section of
'Mystique'. In 'Aube' the layout and the shape of the text express
visually its enigmatic theme, the success and the failure of the
child's pursuit of the dawn goddess. The poem is set between two
short lines of equal length 'J'ai embrassé l'aube d'été' and 'Au
réveil il était midi', suggesting, even representing, the arms of
the child which, having embraced the summer dawn, are powerless to hold it. In the last sentence of 'Mystique', 'la douceur
fleurie des étoiles et du ciel et du reste descend en face du talus,
comme un panier; — contre notre face, et fait l'abîme fleurant
et bleu là-dessous', the words are ordered in such a way that by
their sound and their symmetrical placing to the left and right
of 'panier' ('la douceur', 'là-dessous'; 'fleurie', 'fleurant'; 'en face',
'notre face'; and 'comme', 'contre') they actually appear to shape
the 'figure' of the basket.[25]

The sensuous plenitude and the utter simplicity of that last sentence of 'Mystique' make one realise the inadequacy of the term *poème en prose* to describe the *Illuminations*. The term *poèmes non versifiés*,[26] although somewhat clumsy, more aptly defines their essentially poetic nature, and reminds us of the problems Rimbaud so successfully overcame in giving structural unity to an artistic form that had discarded versification and ready-made frameworks. The *Illuminations* are his greatest achievement and they are the climax of a poetic and human drama to which *Une Saison en enfer* is the dénouement.

7

UNE SAISON EN ENFER

Poésies, Derniers vers or *Vers nouveaux et chansons,* and *Illuminations* are collections or groups of poems which have been arranged in a certain order, and given those titles, by various
editors. *Une Saison en enfer,* on the other hand, is a work which,
from its inception to its publication, was under Rimbaud's control. It was he who decided the order of the nine sections, gave
them their titles, dated the work, found a publisher in Brussels,
corrected the proofs and saw it through the press. As well as
being his only sustained and completed work — his only *œuvre* —
Une Saison en enfer is the work which Rimbaud himself considered, perhaps for personal reasons, of supreme importance.
Some of the sections were written before, and some after the
quarrel in Brussels in which Verlaine shot and wounded him, an
event which may have suggested the title, *Une Saison en enfer,*
in place of the ones originally thought of — 'Livre païen' and
'Livre nègre'.

More is known about *Une Saison en enfer* than about *Poésies* or
the *Illuminations.* We have drafts of three sections, and an inval-
uable letter to Ernest Delahaye, written in May 1873, which
shows Rimbaud at the family farm at Roche, in the act of composing the work which was later to become *Une Saison en enfer.*
The poet's attitude to his work in progress is revealing. He has
already thought about a title, and about the length and the structure of the book: nine 'petites histoires en prose', three of which
he has finished and half-a-dozen he still has to 'faire' or 'inventer'.
The use of these verbs, in particular the second, and his reference
to the stories as 'histoires atroces' and 'atrocités', suggest the
attitude of a writer who is conscious of his craft and of the effect
he hopes to produce. The letter also reveals frenzied activity,
total absorption and a sense of crisis. When Rimbaud declares,
'Mon sort dépend de ce livre', one feels that he is thinking not
only of literary glory but of some kind of human fate or 'salvation'.

Une Saison en enfer can be read as a self-contained narration, with a beginning, a middle and an end, as a work of art complete in itself; but it does not fit neatly into any definite genre. It defies classification, and even today critics are divided, not only about its meaning and the exact nature of its 'hell', but also about its importance and value as a literary text. Like the *Illuminations*, it has been interpreted in widely divergent and even more extreme ways, ranging from a spiritual conversion and a 'return to God', to a rejection of poetry and a 'return to reality'; so that for generations of readers, it has been a Bible or, more often, an anti-Bible. Verlaine, in his enthusiastic uncritical way, probably came nearest to defining its particular nature and style when he wrote, in his article, 'Arthur Rimbaud "1884"', that it was an 'espèce de prodigieuse autobiographie', written in a 'prose de diamant'. Even if the work is not an autobiography in the customary sense and does not tell accurately and in detail the story of Rimbaud's life, it is a comprehensive survey of his beliefs and ambitions. A narrative element is felt in the recurrence of explicit statements, and is heightened by the almost total absence of certain images, notably those of the stage and theatre, which are pervasive in the *Illuminations*. There, they had been used to create a multiplicity of viewpoints and perspectives, suggesting the mind's limitless possibilities. Here, our attention is confined to the actor himself and to emotions and ideas which − at one time projected into imaginary figures and dramas − are now locked in conflict within his own mind. Whereas in the *Illuminations* Rimbaud's spirit was always 'en avant', reaching into the future, in *Une Saison en enfer* the first movement is a turning to the past and a regret for a 'festin'.[1]

The whole of *Une Saison en enfer* is, of course, rooted in the past, in what Rimbaud calls his 'sale éducation d'enfance' and his Catholic upbringing. One of his most profound statements, 'Je suis esclave de mon baptême' in the 'Nuit de l'enfer', is immediately followed by a statement attributing all the blame to his parents: 'Parents, vous avez fait mon malheur et vous avez fait le vôtre. Pauvre innocent!' The same psychological mechanism which we noted in the early poems and in the *Lettre du voyant* is at work in *Une Saison en enfer*. Rimbaud is fascinated by what revolts him; and he is both attracted and repelled by the doctrines of Catholicism. Religious images and expressions constantly recur, but these, like the Latin of the Liturgy to which at times he has recourse (for example, *De profundis Domine* in 'Mauvais sang', *ad matutinum* and *Christus venit* in 'Délires II. Alchimie du verbe', *Pater* and *Ave Maria* in 'Matin'), are ridiculed and dismissed. He still needs what he claims to reject, and his 'slavery' is necessary so that he can affirm his passionate desire for freedom, whether through the dream of a mythical past — a lost paradise or the golden age of youth — or through an aspiration to an idealised and impossible future.

Une Saison en enfer can perhaps be best seen as a dramatised confession, or the parody of a confession, in which Rimbaud is both guilty and innocent, a 'damné' and a 'pauvre innocent'. Yet, in this confession, there is nothing normal, calm or passive; it is an upheaval, a volcanic eruption. Themes that had been suppressed or transcended in the *Illuminations* invade the poet's mind with unparalleled force, and he is suddenly confronted with all the antitheses, antinomies and dualisms which are inherent in the condition of Western man. *Une Saison en enfer* is in fact much more than a confession. It is a spiritual battle in which the protagonists are God and Satan, Good and Evil, Sin and Innocence, Past and Future, the Occident and the Orient, Body and Mind, and at least thirty other antithetical couples. The title, as brilliant a *trouvaille* as Baudelaire's *Les Fleurs du mal*, indicates the nature of the work, the brevity and intensity of the poet's suffering. As the 'ivresse' of the *voyant* had lasted only for a 'matinée', so the anguish is only for a 'saison'; and in the title, 'Saison', the less dramatic of the two words, is the more important. The idea of a 'season' as a part of the year, or a symbolic season of ecstasy, loss or despair, and more generally as a period of time — real time and the poet's emotional time — is present from the first to the last section and, with its store of lyrical associations, is a unifying theme.

Une Saison en enfer has a logical plan and a coherent structure. Even the titles of the sections — 'Mauvais sang', 'Nuit de l'enfer', 'Délires I', 'Délires II', 'L'Impossible', 'L'Éclair', 'Matin', and 'Adieu' — show a concern for an artistic effect, and they delineate the general development and the external structure. This and the inner structure are most clearly seen in the prologue, 'Jadis, si je me souviens bien'; in the long central movement consisting of the two 'délires' ('Vierge folle — L'Époux infernal'

and 'Alchimie du verbe'); and in the conclusion 'Adieu', which
is both a summing up and a dénouement. In each of these sections, an allusion to a season — spring in the prologue, summer
in the 'Délires', autumn and winter in 'Adieu' — marks a significant phase in Rimbaud's 'hell'. *Une Saison en enfer* has often
been seen as an uncontrolled upsurge of ideas and feelings;
but one is as conscious of Rimbaud's art as of the tumultuous
nature of his emotions. The pervasive repetition, for example, of
words, motifs and rhythms, which denotes a frenzied obsession
with certain ideas and states of mind, is also used as a structural
device.

   This balance and sense of structure are felt in the opening
section where, as Ernest Delahaye noted, albeit somewhat fan-
cifully, sentences and paragraphs follow each other 'with the
elegance of a minuet'.[2] This is untitled, and is usually called the
prelude or prologue. It sets the ironic tone and introduces some
of the main themes: childhood, time, duality, suffering, death.
Above all, it indicates, in the first two sentences, where the
stress will fall throughout the work: first on life, in particular
Rimbaud's own life ('ma vie était un festin où s'ouvraient tous
les cœurs, où tous les vins coulaient'), and then on literature,
especially his own poetry and poetic beliefs ('Un soir, j'ai assis
la Beauté sur mes genoux. — Et je l'ai trouvée amère. — Et je
l'ai injuriée'). Always, literature is secondary and is seen in
terms of life. The reference to Beauty is reminiscent of the
passage in the second section of Vigny's 'La Maison du ber-
ger', where he attacks those who have defiled the Muse of
poetry ('un vieillard, t'enivrant de son baiser jaloux,/Releva
le premier ta robe de prêtresse,/Et, parmi les garçons, t'assit
sur ses genoux'). The image may be similar, but the sense is
different; and Rimbaud rejects what Vigny had always defended, namely, a moral and didactic view of poetry, 'perle de la
Pensée'.
   This introductory section prepares the stage for the beginning
of a battle or drama, in which Rimbaud directs his attack against
moral virtues and normal human emotions. Brutal sado-maso-
chistic sentences express feelings that surge from one extreme
to another; and a savage thrust at the external world and its
values is immediately followed by self-laceration and a desire

for punishment:

> Je me suis armé contre la justice.
>
> Je me suis enfui. Ô sorcières, ô misère, ô haine, c'est à vous que mon trésor a été confié!
>
> Je parvins à faire s'évanouir dans mon esprit toute l'espérance humaine. Sur toute joie pour l'étrangler j'ai fait le bond sourd de la bête féroce.
>
> J'ai appelé les bourreaux pour, en périssant, mordre la crosse de leurs fusils. J'ai appelé les fléaux, pour m'étouffer avec le sable, le sang. Le malheur a été mon dieu. Je me suis allongé dans la boue. Je me suis séché à l'air du crime.

These violent, yet controlled, fluctuations are characteristic of the whole work, as are the two roles which Rimbaud adopts. He is both the 'bête féroce' ('hyène', Satan calls him) and at the same time, as is evident from his bantering address to the Devil, the detached cynical observer. But he is also the poet, a different one from the *voyant* who, in the *Illuminations*, had proudly proclaimed that he had discovered 'quelque chose comme la clef de l'amour'. Now, referring to the incident in Brussels when he imagined himself on the point of death ('tout dernièrement m'étant trouvé sur le point de faire le dernier *couae!*'), he is preoccupied with finding again 'la clef du festin ancien'. Charity, which might be the key, is at once rejected because of its Christian associations, and satirised as an 'inspiration'. Statement followed by counter-statement, affirmation by denial, acceptance by rejection, may be the sign of a profound spiritual conflict, but it is also a conscious literary device which enables Rimbaud to examine, criticise and attack opposed attitudes, and to reveal absurdities in established values. In the same way Time, the most inexorable of the antagonists, is used as a structural device to give the work coherence and unity. 'Jadis' opens the section; and 'le printemps' divides it into equal parts, the first dealing with a remote, imagined past, and the second with a recent past and also with the present, when Rimbaud has become aware of good and evil and the many other dualities in life.

The prologue recalls 'Au Lecteur', Baudelaire's preface to *Les Fleurs du mal*; but Rimbaud adopts a different, perverse convention, addressing not the reader but himself and Satan —

to whom he appropriately offers his work in ironic homage:

> Mais, cher Satan, ... vous qui aimez dans l'écrivain l'absence des facultés descriptives ou instructives, je vous détache ces quelques hideux feuillets de mon carnet de damné.

He flatters Satan by attributing to him literary tastes, and the flattery is the more subtle because these are precisely the tastes to which Rimbaud's own best work bears witness: absence of description and of didacticism. The absence of these two features characterises the *Illuminations*, for example in 'Jeunesse' the 'voix instructives' are exiled, and in 'Vies' the poet asks, 'Qu'at-on fait du brahmane qui m'expliqua les Proverbes?' Yet in *Une Saison en enfer* there *is* description, not it is true of the external world, but of the poet's own mind, and inevitably the meaning of the work becomes 'instructive' not only for Rimbaud but also for the reader.

In the prologue, as elsewhere, Rimbaud's attitude to Satan is equivocal. He allies himself with the arch-rebel the better to express his defiance of Christ; but as his damnation is only for a season, he can, at the same time, taunt and provoke him, and finally show him to be a myth, or, to borrow Renan's expression, an 'excellent fiction'. Later, he uses Christ in the same ambiguous way. In 'Nuit de l'enfer', for example, he identifies himself with Him, assuming His role, and paraphrasing His words, but only in order to undermine the belief in His divinity: 'Fiez-vous donc à moi ... Tous, venez, — même les petits enfants ... Je ne demande pas de prières; avec votre confiance seulement, je serai heureux.' Again, in 'Délires I. Vierge folle—L'Époux infernal', based on the parable of the ten foolish virgins, the perverse identification of the 'Époux infernal' with the heavenly bridegroom is used to parody and destroy the belief in the divinity of Christ. This identification, first with Satan then with Christ, the extremes of evil and good, followed by mockery and rejection, reflects Rimbaud's search for a solution acceptable on his own terms. But he is equally equivocal towards himself, and as he constantly eludes any rational examination of his dilemma — 'Je suis caché et je ne le suis pas', he says in 'Nuit de l'enfer' — it is difficult to be certain that his solution is not another 'attitude' or evasion. That uncertainty, which has made possible so many varied interpretations of *Une Saison en enfer*, does not however in any way diminish our appreciation of the extraordinary skill and beauty of Rimbaud's ambiguous art.

The sweeping, dogmatic statements of an essentially personal kind used in the prologue (only one sentence is impersonal: 'La charité est cette clef') are one of the most obvious features of *Une Saison en enfer*. In the next section, 'Mauvais sang', however, one becomes conscious of a more subtle feature — the occasional use of an impersonal statement at an important point in the text: for instance, 'La main à plume vaut la main à charrue', 'Le monde marche! Pourquoi ne tournerait-il pas?', 'L'amour divin seul octroie les clefs de la science', 'La vie est la farce à mener par tous.' This strategic placing of impersonal, epigrammatic statements among predominantly personal utterances is a means Rimbaud adopts to give an ordered pattern to the expression of a disordered mind. Moreover, as well as telling about himself, it enables him to comment on the human condition and so give universality to his work.

Delahaye's word 'menuet' may not be the most appropriate term to describe the prologue; but 'Mauvais sang', consisting of numerous interwoven variations on a single theme, could be likened to a fugue. The 'mauvais sang' is 'le sang païen', the blood which is the sign of Rimbaud's innocence because, through no fault of his, he is a heathen; and the sign of his guilt, because he is not a Christian. As the blood circulates and returns — 'le sang païen revient!', he exclaims — it brings images of other blood, and of salvation through sacrifice. Rimbaud begins by making his ancestors, the barbaric Gauls, responsible for his faults, vices and sins; and for his being 'race inférieure'. They were destroyers, and their stupid descendants had infected the earth with materialism, reason, nineteenth-century positivism, so-called progress and science, ironically described as 'la nouvelle noblesse'. As the poet recalls the history of France, he sees himself in many roles, but always as an alien and an outcast — serf, leper, mercenary, convict, savage, negro. In his imagination, he has been everywhere, seen and known everything; but he is rootless, 'toujours seul, sans famille'. In a desperate longing for a true spiritual nobility, he turns momentarily to Christianity and thinks of the Holy Ghost, Christ, the Gospel, and God. 'J'attends Dieu avec gourmandise', he declares, and while waiting, he finds consolation in thinking of conventional success, with values acceptable to society: virility, money, women, politics. 'Sauvé!' he mockingly exclaims, and then, without transition, he returns to his present state — 'maudit' — and to a desire, viewed sardonically, for oblivion in a drunken sleep. In the next passage, realising that no escape is possible and that the conflict cannot be disposed of by sleep, he appears to accept the burden of his sin and his human condition, 'Allons! La marche, le fardeau, le désert, l'ennui et la colère ... La vie dure ...' — a statement to which his life was later to give reality. But simplification by action is no more efficacious than forgetfulness through sleep. The repressed torment breaks through in a series of questions which reveal the extent of Rimbaud's solitude and the disordered state of his mind:

> À qui me louer? Quelle bête faut-il adorer? Quelle sainte image attaque-t-on? Quels cœurs briserai-je? Quel mensonge dois-je tenir? — Dans quel sang marcher?

Torn between extremes, 'le ciel' and 'ici-bas', he thinks again of charity and the Christian virtues. This solution is rejected as soon as it is entertained, and he exclaims: 'De profundis Domine, suis-je bête!' Invariably, anything associated with religion is followed by savage dismissal; a longing for God being the surest proof of weakness and degradation.

In the fifth part of 'Mauvais sang', Rimbaud plays out in dramatic form several complementary themes: guilt and innocence, damnation and salvation, passivity and aggression, masochism and sadism, etc. He recalls the time when, as a child, he had felt so alienated from society that he had identified himself with the convict, like him an outcast and a rebel, seeing towns and 'civilised' life through his eyes and with his mentality. On winter nights his suffering left him with a death-like appearance which by morning made him almost unrecognisable to those he met: 'Au matin j'avais le regard si perdu et la contenance si morte, que ceux que j'ai rencontrés ne m'ont peut-être pas vu.' Then, as though extreme privation had quickened the senses and produced enrichment, the outcast with 'le regard si perdu' suddenly sees with the eyes of the voyant, and the narrative is interrupted by a passage leading through a series of images to an apocalyptic vision:

> Dans les villes la boue m'apparaissait soudainement rouge
> et noire, comme une glace quand la lampe circule dans la
> chambre voisine, comme un trésor dans la forêt! Bonne
> chance, criais-je, et je voyais une mer de flammes et de fu-
> mée au ciel; et, à gauche, à droite, toutes les richesses flam-
> bant comme un milliard de tonnerres.

This extract is similar to the evocation in the fifth section of
'Enfance' of the 'ville monstrueuse', the town where the mud is
'rouge ou noire'; but it has a closer resemblance to another of the
Illuminations, 'Mystique', where there is a similar 'situating' of
the scene ('À gauche le terreau de l'arête ... Derrière l'arête de
droite ...'), and a similar fiery vision ('Des prés de flammes bon-
dissent jusqu'au sommet du mamelon ...'). But the scene in
'Mauvais sang' is the demonic counterpart of 'Mystique', with
fire no longer just part of a unified verbal pattern, but dominant and destructive of 'toutes les richesses'. Moments of imagery
and vision such as this are relatively rare in *Une Saison en enfer*
which is, as Rimbaud himself says in 'Matin', a 'relation', a
narration. In a draft version of 'Nuit de l'enfer' he is more explicit: 'Puis-je décrire la vision, on n'est pas poète en enfer'; and in
the final text: 'Puis-je décrire la vision, l'air de l'enfer ne souffre
pas les hymnes!' Even images of fire, which one might expect
to be numerous in the scenario and story of this period in hell,
are infrequent; and their appearance at this point is not only
unexpected but significant. The effect of surprise and suddenness, conveyed by both verb — 'apparaissait' — and adverb —
'soudainement' — is followed by a rapid expansion of space from
a 'chambre' to a 'forêt' to a 'mer de flammes et de fumée au ciel',
from the confined and familiar to the vast and strange — a *fluid*
conflagration. In 'mer de flammes', water and fire unite to evoke
a Dante-like inferno, as, later, at the end of 'Nuit de l'enfer', the
same two elements are fused in a minute, but equally original
image, 'une goutte de feu'. These are two examples of how one,
or more, of the four elements — earth, water, air, fire — can
nourish and re-energise the poetic imagination, as Gaston
Bachelard has shown.[3] They have a special significance in

Une Saison en enfer, where water and fire symbolise not only baptism and hell, but also transformation and regeneration.

Again Rimbaud returns to the solitude of his childhood:

> Pas même un compagnon. Je me voyais devant une foule exaspérée, en face du peloton d'exécution, pleurant du malheur qu'ils n'aient pu comprendre, et pardonnant! — Comme Jeanne d'Arc! — «Prêtres, professeurs, maîtres, vous vous trompez en me livrant à la justice. Je n'ai jamais été de ce peuple-ci; je n'ai jamais été chrétien; je suis de la race qui chantait dans le supplice; je ne comprends pas les lois; je n'ai pas le sens moral, je suis une brute: vous vous trompez ...»
>
> Oui, j'ai les yeux fermés à votre lumière. Je suis une bête, un nègre. Mais je puis être sauvé. Vous êtes de faux nègres, vous maniaques, féroces, avares. Marchand, tu es nègre; magistrat, tu es nègre; général, tu es nègre; empereur, vieille démangeaison, tu es nègre ...

Like Joan of Arc, also a rebel, he is condemned to death for his visions. In protesting his innocence, he attacks those who have judged and sentenced him — priests, teachers, merchants, magistrates, generals — all, like his 'Homme juste', hypocrites and pillars of a Christian society. And he asserts that they are mistaken in their condemnation because he does not belong to their race, has never been a Christian, and so cannot be judged by standards and laws he does not accept. This obsession with innocence, suffering and martyrdom is a complex and ambiguous theme, and the negro who embodies it represents both primitive man in his purity, the noble savage, and the unclean, guilty child. Rimbaud feels, however, that he himself is the true primitive and so may yet be saved. His judges and executioners, on the other hand, are 'faux nègres' who, by the 'light' of their reason, have misunderstood him. They are the adults who have betrayed the visionary light of childhood which he, at least in his poetry, has preserved intact. Despite the over-emphasis, and the melodramatic nature of the scene, this is one of the moments in *Une Saison en enfer* where Rimbaud's vehement attack is convincing, and where the 'je' takes on more than personal significance and becomes representative of the individual in his struggle against an uncomprehending and corrupt society.

The revolt is followed by disgust, and he thinks of leaving Europe, but finds instead a more profound escape in a return to a physical elemental state, and an ecstasy of forgetfulness through gesture and action: 'Faim, soif, cris, danse, danse, danse, danse!'

In the next passage, he presents in two images a simplified version of the main theme of salvation and damnation. The first image is of the white race landing from their ship to 'save' him by forcing him at the point of the gun to be baptised. The other is of a 'navire sauveur', the ship of salvation, symbol of divine love, which, dispensing with military formalities, rescues him, but leaves the others, his friends, to drown. The ironic presentation (reminiscent of the shipwreck incident in the fifth chapter of Voltaire's *Candide*), the contrasts and similarities between these two orders and two kinds of love, human and divine, make one realise that if Rimbaud were to accept salvation it would be on his own terms. Nevertheless, he decides that, for the time being, he will love his fellow men and praise God. But again, no sooner has he accepted this salvation than he rejects it and demands the impossible, 'la liberté dans le salut'. Nothing must constrain his spirit, yet innocent or guilty, he is obliged to accept, with the rest of us, the inescapable burden of life itself; and in an aphoristic statement he expresses his philosophy of the Absurd: 'La vie est la farce à mener par tous.' The farce is then illustrated in the conclusion by a satirical picture of Rimbaud seeking salvation in the despised French way of life — as a soldier facing death in battle.

'Nuit de l'enfer' which, as we know from the draft, had originally been called 'Fausse Conversion' (perhaps too obvious a key to the meaning) begins with the statement 'J'ai avalé une fameuse gorgée de poison.' In tone and style, this beginning is typical. By this kind of short sentence, with a normal word order of subject, verb, object, Rimbaud achieves some of his most forceful and sardonic effects. The physical and mental results of this 'poison' seem to bring the full realisation that he is enduring hell fire and eternal damnation. The poison which is ironically welcomed and blessed at the beginning, is, at the end, equated with a kiss, 'ce baiser mille fois maudit'; and whereas the 'mauvais sang' was the blood of the heathen, the kiss is the poison of

Christianity, the 'Baiser putride de Jésus' of 'Les Premières communions'. Rimbaud is, as he himself puts it, the slave of his baptism. In 'Mauvais sang', he referred to the 'chant raisonnable' of the angels and declared, 'la raison m'est née'; but now he has moved into an irrational realm of darkness and hallucinations, an ostensibly deeper experience, which he views with detachment and irony. The hell which is portrayed is mocked in a parody of Cartesian logic, 'Je me crois en enfer, donc j'y suis.' This melodramatic section, beginning and ending with poison, fire and damnation, is like a mosaic or synthesis of parodies – of the mystic's Dark Night of the Soul, Dante's *Inferno* and a Catholic version of Hell. 'La théologie est sérieuse, l'enfer est certainement *en bas* – et le ciel en haut', says Rimbaud, and to show how 'serious' he is, he affirms, 'Je brûle comme il faut.' Throughout this long soliloquy, more than anywhere else in *Une Saison en enfer*, he is the actor conscious of the effect he wishes to create through tone of voice, asides, studied gestures, and 'toutes les grimaces imaginables'. By the same means, he peoples the stage of his solitude with spectres from his past, and the principal figures of the Christian drama, the Devil, God, Christ, the Virgin Mary.

He makes repeated appeals to his audience to look – 'Voyez comme le feu se relève!'; to agree – 'Un homme qui veut se mutiler est bien damné, n'est-ce pas?'; to keep away – 'Qu'on n'approche pas'; to listen – 'Écoutez!'; to reply – 'Veut-on des chants nègres, des danses de houris?'; and to have faith in him (and here he identifies himself with Christ) – 'Fiez-vous donc à moi . . . tous, venez, même les petits enfants . . .'. The final appeal is to God, 'Mon Dieu, pitié, cachez-moi, je me tiens trop mal.' Here, Rimbaud plays on two meanings of 'se tenir' – his behaviour as a human being, and his bearing as an actor, which have both been bad because his attitude has been equivocal and, as he says in the next sentence, because he has neither concealed nor revealed himself. Like the ideal actor of Diderot's *Paradoxe sur le comédien*, he has tried to hide his real feelings, but some of the roles he has attempted to portray have not yet been written and cannot therefore be learned and imitated. Moreover, he has suddenly been confronted with a new element in the drama, 'l'Orgueil', his own besetting sin and, according to Saint Gregory the Great, the general commanding the devil's army of deadly sins.

'Mauvais sang' showed the individual opposed to society as a whole. 'Nuit de l'enfer' shows him in conflict with its moral values and religious beliefs. Special emphasis is given to Pride because this is one of the causes of his present hell, and the source of his human and literary ambitions. 'Nobles ambitions', he exclaims ironically, and later says, 'Je vais dévoiler tous les mystères: mystères religieux ou naturels, mort, naissance, avenir, passé, cosmogonie, néant. Je suis maître en fantasmagories ... J'ai tous les talents ...'. The naturalness and the poignancy of cries which spring from the memory of childhood, such as, 'Ah! l'enfance, l'herbe, la pluie, le lac sur les pierres ...', emphasise not only the artificiality of his posturing but also what lies beneath it, namely, the desperate need to find a way out of his dilemma. The lucid, if cynical, realisation of his overweening pride leads directly to a detailed appraisal in the next two sections, 'Délires I' and 'Délires II'; and points the way to a resolution, or at least an 'attitude', that is finally reached in 'Adieu', the concluding section.

'Délires' is the centre and climax of *Une Saison en enfer*; and, in structural terms, it forms the keystone of the work. It consists of two parts, 'Vierge folle—L'Époux infernal' and 'Alchimie du verbe'; and if the experience described in them can be qualified as 'delirious', it is a delirium controlled and mastered by art. Despite the title, this is the most objective and the most rigorously constructed of all the sections. To change the metaphor, 'Délires' resembles a diptych with one panel depicting the Infernal Bridegroom (Rimbaud), his life and human ambitions, and his relationship with the Foolish Virgin (Verlaine); and the other portraying his literary ideals, illustrated by examples taken from his own poetry. Both are pictures of failure; but they are presented in so many varying lights and analysed with such penetrating detail that they are among Rimbaud's most brilliant achievements. The rigour and the beauty of the composition are evident not only in each separate 'délire' but also in their reciprocal relationships, the literary failure contrasting with, and at the same time illustrating, the human failure.

After a long monologue addressed to an imaginary companion, the Devil, Rimbaud introduces into his hell a 'real' companion; a device which gives the work a human quality, and

greater narrative and dramatic potentiality. The first of the
'délires', based on the parable of the Foolish Virgins, is a confession — and the parody of a confession — within the general
confessional framework of *Une Saison en enfer*. While seeing
Verlaine with the utmost clarity, Rimbaud sees himself looking
at Verlaine, who in turn is looking at him; and at the same time
he sees Verlaine looking at both of them in their homosexual
relationship. As the creator and script-writer of this drama,
Rimbaud could say, as Monsieur Teste does in Valéry's *La
Soirée avec Monsieur Teste*, 'Je suis étant, et me voyant; me voyant
me voir, et ainsi de suite . . .'. As far as one can judge from available sources, in particular Verlaine's letters to Rimbaud and the
numerous poems in which he alludes to himself, Rimbaud has
caught every trait of his character: the sentimentality, the plead-
ing, the weeping, the self-pity, the religiosity, the childishness,
the passivity, the dependence, the helplessness of mind and
body, the fear and the bewilderment, the incomprehension, even
the tone of his insinuating voice. In a sentence, Rimbaud has
summed up Verlaine's desertion of wife and child, and the
tragedy of his life: 'J'ai oublié tout mon devoir humain pour le
suivre.' But the portrait, as well as being cruel and sadistic, is
incomplete and one-sided. There is no hint of the other Verlaine,
the poet, only the Verlaine whom Claudel, in his poem 'Verlaine', was to describe as 'faible', 'lamentable' and an 'espèce de
soudard immonde'.

In 'Vierge folle—L'Époux infernal', Verlaine is seen as the
Foolish Virgin enslaved by Catholicism, torn between a love
of God, the 'divin Époux', and a desire for Rimbaud, the 'Époux
infernal'. Weak and helpless, he is tossed to and fro, as in the
'bon délire' of his own poem, 'Le Bon Disciple'. At various
points in Verlaine's confession, which typically is often a maud-
lin 'confidence', Rimbaud puts into the mouth of his companion
words and phrases similar to those he has previously used about
himself. This simple verbal artifice is an unusually effective
means of emphasising the extent of Verlaine's submissive-
ness, which is evident throughout the section. In addition, by
making slight but significant changes, such as the omission of a
forceful adjective, adverb, or image, Rimbaud 'dilutes' Verlaine's language, so that the Foolish Virgin's suffering is expressed in a series of enfeebled, prosaic statements, which

reveal fundamental differences in the intensity, quality, and even in the 'temperature' of the reactions of the two partners. The Foolish Virgin's exclamation, 'Ah! je souffre, je crie. Je souffre vraiment', expresses the suffering of a weak and submissive character; whereas, in 'Nuit de l'enfer', Rimbaud re-enacts his anguish in virile, masculine language which is itself a liberating force: 'Les entrailles me brûlent. La violence du venin tord mes membres, me rend difforme, me terrasse.'

A particularly interesting passage (put in quotation marks to indicate that the words are those of the Infernal Bridegroom as reported by the Foolish Virgin) refers back to what Rimbaud had said in 'Jadis' and at the beginning of 'Mauvais sang' about his barbarous ancestors. Retransmitted through the mind of the Foolish Virgin, everything is confused, facts are inaccurate, and actions either exaggerated or trivialised; for example, the Gauls who buttered their hair become Scandinavians who drank their own blood. Rimbaud, who had declared, 'J'ai appelé les fléaux, pour m'étouffer avec le sable, le sang', is made to utter the absurdity, '"je me tatouerai ... je ramperais [a characteristic Verlaine verb of action] et me tordrais sur le tapis"'; and his image 'Je n'aurais jamais ma main' becomes the flat statement '"Jamais je ne travaillerai."' This passage illustrates one of the main functions of the Foolish Virgin persona: purgation through ridicule and a fearless, lucid vision. While satirising the Foolish Virgin's muddled mind and the masochistic need to see the Infernal Bridegroom as a terrifying figure, the device also enables the Infernal Bridegroom to see again and criticise, in a different perspective, his own ideas and actions. Similarly, the Foolish Virgin is made to report in 'her' own words some of the Infernal Bridegroom's ideas about social questions, such as the dependent position of woman in society and man's attitude towards her:

'Tu vois cet élégant jeune homme, entrant dans la belle et calme maison: il s'appelle Duval, Dufour, Armand, Maurice, que sais-je? Une femme s'est dévouée à aimer ce méchant idiot: elle est morte, c'est certes une sainte au ciel, à présent.'

That passage, apparently casual and offhand, sums up with merciless clarity social attitudes and a whole ethos. It is also an ironic comment on Rimbaud's own attitude, on the apathy and cynicism which, because of the relationship with Verlaine, had overtaken him since the time of the *Lettre du voyant*. Then, he had prophesied that woman's endless servitude would be broken so that she too could become a person in her own right, even a poet, and discover the new and the unknown.

Despite pious utterance about God, and tears of penitence, the Foolish Virgin is concerned only with this world, its opinions and values, and, above all, with self and carnal satisfactions. 'Her' horizon is so limited that, while being totally dependent on the Infernal Bridegroom, 'she' is unable to understand him; the bewildered questions about his wish to escape from reality and to change life reveal chasms of incomprehension. 'J'ignore son idéal', 'she' concludes. 'She' believes that, without any effort, a new life, virile and adventurous, will be given 'her' as a present to a child; or that one day, on awaking from sleep, she will find, thanks to the Infernal Bridegroom's magic power, that laws and customs have changed and that she will be free to satisfy every whim and desire. Even when the Infernal Bride-groom demonstrates some of his ideas, his actions are as mis-construed as his thoughts; yet, in spite of apparent weaknesses and limitations, the Foolish Virgin, with shrewd feminine intuition, sees through him and judges him: 'Il feignait d'être éclairé sur tout, commerce, art, médecine.' She knows that his omnipotence was only a pretence, and that he was still searching for what he claimed to possess already, namely, secrets for changing life: 'Il a peut-être des secrets pour *changer la vie*? Non, il ne fait qu'en chercher, me répliquais-je.' This insight is all the more ironic because the image of the Foolish Virgin was obviously inspired by Rimbaud's disgust at Verlaine's inability to understand anything about his ideas, aims, and ideals, an inability paralleled by Rimbaud's own failure to understand, until too late, Verlaine. He sees in him not only the example of an abject, irredeemable human being, but also his own image as a failed prophet and *voyant*. If he could not change Verlaine, how could he change life? This first 'délire', although osten-sibly objective, expresses Rimbaud's personal involvement, and reflects in dramatic form the conflicts of his divided nature. If on one level, the Foolish Virgin is Verlaine, on another, 'she' is Rimbaud's projection of the passive 'feminine' half of his own personality. In many ways 'Délires I' is a masterpiece of indirect self-confession because, in making the Foolish Virgin confess, the Infernal Bridegroom also confesses.

Rimbaud's presentation of himself as the highly ambiguous figure of the Infernal Bridegroom raises many questions. Is the Infernal Bridegroom a portrait of himself seen through Verlaine's eyes? Or does it serve a double purpose and give also a self-portrait, concealed beneath the mask of the supposedly fictional character? Or is the Infernal Bridegroom a more complex and equivocal figure, a mixture of Rimbaud's own ideas about himself and those of Verlaine about him, to which are added elements of a fantasy figure, half-demon, half-angel, which Rimbaud has created in response to his own and Verlaine's eccentric desires and satisfactions?

Having considered how Rimbaud makes Verlaine, as the Foolish Virgin, see him in his fictional guise of the Infernal Bridegroom, it is revealing to look at some of Verlaine's poems in which it can be seen how Verlaine in turn, and in other contexts, sees Rimbaud. The agreement between the two portraits is remarkable. Every detail in 'Délires I' has its parallel in a Verlaine text: Rimbaud's strange beauty ('très beau d'une beauté paysanne et rusée'); his adolescence and his rage ('cet enfant de colère'); his strength and virility ('un Hercule'); his posturings and grimaces ('viles simagrées'); his arrogance and his gestures ('de satyre'); and, above all, the two poles of his nature ('Ange ET Démon'). The 'nuits de noce' of 'Le Poète et la Muse', and the 'roman de vivre à deux hommes', so joyfully recounted in 'Laeti et errabundi', are the ironic counterpart of the concubinage in hell. For Verlaine, Rimbaud is his 'grand péché radieux'.[4]

In 'Délires I', the Foolish Virgin and the Infernal Bridegroom express in concrete and dramatic form a struggle which has previously been carried on between Rimbaud and abstract antagonists. These two fictional figures, at once insignificant and tremendous, stand out against a vast context, and they throw lights of evil and of good backwards and forwards over the whole work. The Foolish Virgin expresses 'her' feelings about the relationship in an image of a place which emphasises the sense of isolation and loneliness, 'J'étais dans son âme comme dans un palais qu'on a vidé pour ne pas voir une personne si peu noble que vous.' The Infernal Bridegroom expresses his isolation and indifference with a shrug of the shoulders; and finally, with an ironic exclamation, a masterpiece of understatement, the relationship is dismissed as a 'Drôle de ménage!'. In rejecting it, he reveals, in a grotesque and perverted way, the pathos and tragedy of a human situation, with the dreams and fantasies of each of the partners, the frustrated aspirations, the impossibility of communication, the misunderstandings and conflicts, and the ultimate loneliness of the individual as each uses the other in a search for some kind of salvation.

In 'Délires II' ('Alchimie du verbe'), Rimbaud considers what he feels to be equally 'drôle': his poetic ambitions, his verbal alchemy, and the influence this revolutionary poetic activity had had on his life. As if relieved at having finished with alibis, personae, and the 'folie' of the Foolish Virgin, he turns to himself, 'À moi. L'histoire d'une de mes folies'. From the literary point of view, this is the most interesting of all the sections. Although more personal than the previous 'délire', it is just as dramatic, for Rimbaud has replaced the Foolish Virgin by a fresh protagonist: his own poetry. At intervals, he introduces, with minor changes, seven of the verse poems composed in May and June 1872: 'Larme' ('Loin des oiseaux . . .'), 'Chanson de la plus haute tour', 'Fêtes de la faim' ('Faim'), 'Le loup criait sous les feuilles', 'L'Éternité' ('Elle est retrouvée'), 'Ô Saison, ô châteaux!'. This use of specimens from his own work is reminiscent of a similar technique in the *Lettre du voyant*, where they illustrated the birth of a new *art poétique*. Here, however, they represent the literary failure of his ideal to find a language, just as in the previous section the Foolish Virgin embodied the human failure to change life. It is possible that Rimbaud chose these particular poems rather than, for example, 'Le Dormeur du val', 'Ophélie', or 'Le Buffet', because they represent a crucial and transitional phase in his evolution between the early verse poems in stanza form and the prose poems of the *Illuminations*, when he was experimenting with what Verlaine termed verses that were 'délicieusement faux exprès'.

Rimbaud's attitude to these naive lyrics and 'romances' is

ambiguous and the attention they receive suggests that, although half-ironically, he is exhibiting with a certain pride what he also condemns. Visually and rhythmically, the poems form a contrast within the text. The effect is a kind of *trompe l'œil* for, although functioning as a background to the prose commentary, they stand out in relief from it; and by their apparent calm and freshness they both counterbalance and heighten the anguish of the poet's self-criticism. All seven are related to the sources of Rimbaud's poetry, and they mark stages or 'seasons' in his development from poet to *voyant*. Although they are used to illustrate the past, all, except the first, evoke a present moment — an eternal present — whether of ecstatic joy ('Elle est retrouvée! Quoi? L'éternité') or of suffering ('le supplice est sûr'). There is, in fact, a subtle interplay between the time when the poems were written (a recent past, but treated as remote), the tenses used in them (mainly the present), and the tenses in the prose text which, though obviously more recent, are almost entirely in the past. In the prose commentary, Rimbaud examines in a measured and logical way the claims he had made in the *Lettre du voyant*, and his achievements since that time. He is now as ironical and contemptuous towards himself and his poetic work as he had been, only two years before, towards his predecessors and contemporaries. He sees his earlier claims as arrogant, and his attempts at visionary poetry a failure. As he is now dealing with concrete particularities (at least when talking about his own poems) rather than metaphysical problems, his 'confession' has the touch and feel of sincerity. More self-critical than elsewhere in *Une Saison en enfer*, he realises, but without any accompanying suggestion of penitence, that he has been guilty, not only of self-deception, but also of bluff and falsity. He recalls that, at the beginning of his career, he had revolted against the generally accepted values of modern art and had found all sources of inspiration within himself; or in things outmoded, commonplace, strange, childlike, that had been neglected or not even noticed by the famous and the philistines:

Depuis longtemps je me vantais de posséder tous les paysages possibles, et trouvais dérisoires les célébrités de la peinture et de la poésie moderne.

J'aimais les peintures idiotes, dessus de portes, décors, toiles de saltimbanques, enseignes, enluminures populaires; la littérature démodée, latin d'église, livres érotiques sans orthographe, romans de nos aïeules; contes de fées, petits livres de l'enfance, opéras vieux, refrains niais, rhythmes naïfs.

This rediscovery of the childlike and the primitive was regarded by André Breton as one of Rimbaud's most challenging and exalting statements, and in it the Surrealists found some of their main themes.

Then, in a short passage which echoes themes in 'Les Poètes de sept ans' and 'Le Bateau ivre', Rimbaud tells of ranging through time and space in dreams of evasion and revolt, of visions of social and geographical upheavals, of his belief in all enchantments. Coming to his actual achievements, he makes a reference to the sonnet 'Voyelles', and to his experiments with vowels, consonants, rhythms: 'J'inventai la couleur des voyelles! – *A* noir, *E* blanc, *I* rouge, *O* bleu, *U* vert. – Je réglai la forme et le mouvement de chaque consonne, et, avec des rhythmes instinctifs, je me flattai d'inventer un verbe poétique accessible, un jour ou l'autre, à tous les sens.' The statement makes it clear that 'Voyelles' had been part of his aim to find a rational and sensuous language which would be more fully and more directly 'accessible' to everyone than any previous means of communication – a communication of meanings and also a communication to all the senses ('sens' here has a double meaning). Rimbaud realises too that the sonnet 'Voyelles' was a part, perhaps the very basis, of his most exciting and humanitarian vision. He now considers all that a mystification; but, as the self-defensive mockery shows, he is only too aware that in deriding vowels, consonants and rhythms he is attacking the poet's raw material, the elements of language itself. Three rapid sentences reflect the speed of his passage from experiments and study to capturing in words silence, night, delirium, and the inexpressible. These are followed by quoting in full, and not quite accurately, possibly because from memory, two of the 1872 verse poems, 'Larme' and 'Bonne pensée du matin' (here not titled). These make an effective contrast, the first being a lyric about the poet himself, and the second, more general and social, about workers. Taken together, the poems illustrate several of the sources and themes that Rimbaud has enumerated and, because of their rhymes and stanza form, they may also be intended to serve as examples of his statement: 'La vieillerie poétique avait une bonne part dans mon alchimie du verbe.' He continues:

Je m'habituai à l'hallucination simple : je voyais très franchement une mosquée à la place d'une usine, une école de tambours faite par des anges, des calèches sur les routes du ciel, un salon au fond d'un lac; les monstres, les mystères; un titre de vaudeville dressait des épouvantes devant moi.

Puis j'expliquai mes sophismes magiques avec l'hallucination des mots!

Je finis par trouver sacré le désordre de mon esprit.

In those statements, all in a past tense, Rimbaud reviews briefly in a logical order, three phases or aspects of his poetry and *art poétique*: first 'la vieillerie poétique', that is, the poems written before the *Illuminations*; next the poetry of his *voyance* — the seeing of visions, 'L'hallucination simple'; and lastly their expression in words, 'L'hallucination des mots'.

'Vieillerie' — 'out-of-date', 'old fashioned' — is pejorative, and suggests contempt for the type of lyrical poetry in rhymed stanza form, such as the 1872 verse poems (of which he has just given two examples), as well as for the earlier more conventional pieces of 1870. In thinking of these early periods, he may also be experiencing some of the affection and nostalgia with which, in 'Le Buffet' (1870), he viewed the jumble of interesting old objects, the 'fouillis de vieilles vieilleries'.

The examples he gives of 'l'hallucination simple' illustrate the nature of his first and simplest visions, passively received or deliberately induced, in which one object replaced another, or was suddenly transformed, or appeared in an unexpected place or context. In the first example, where a mosque takes the place of a factory, the link between word and object has been severed and the purely representational function of the word destroyed; yet, by the very fact of their being mentioned, they 'exist' together and suggest some of the extremes in *Une Saison en enfer* and in Rimbaud's life: religion and materialism, East and West, two irreconcilable civilisations or worlds. In 'Une école de

tambours faite par des anges', drummers are replaced by angels;
but the 'school' remains as a link between them, as does the
idea of music. The vision is therefore more stable and less ar-
resting than the previous one. These angel musicians, although
playing unusual instruments, remind us of those we already
know from paintings and carvings, and so cause little more than
amused surprise. They have none of the liberating impact of the
drum image in one of the *Illuminations*: 'Un coup de ton doigt
sur le tambour décharge tous les sons et commence la nouvelle
harmonie' ('À une raison'). Yet this transformation of the
ordinary, and in particular the placing of the heavenly in an
everyday human context, is characteristic of Rimbaud's visionary techniques. The next two examples, 'des calèches sur les
routes du ciel' and 'un salon au fond d'un lac', may be allusions
to the *Illuminations*, the first to 'Nocturne vulgaire' (but the
relationship is tenuous), the second to 'Soir historique' ('on joue
aux cartes au fond de l'étang'). But, more important, these are
the kinds of visions that characterise the anti-natural, upside-
down world of the *Illuminations*, where a cathedral comes down,
and a lake rises up. Critics have suggested that the 'vaudeville'
mentioned in the last example may be Scribe's comedy, *Michel
et Christine*, a title which Rimbaud had used for one of his 1872
verse poems. The example has, however, a more general significance in showing how a banal or incongruous source, perhaps in this case a poster, could act upon the poet's over-
wrought mind. One thinks of Apollinaire who later found a
lyrical beauty (without any accompanying terror) in 'les
prospectus les catalogues les affiches qui chantent tout haut'
('Zone').

   Rimbaud quickly realised, however, that to translate hallucinatory visions by hallucinatory words was to be caught in the
magic web of a new convention, and to turn in a vicious circle.
The poetic method he had formulated in the *Lettre du voyant*
as a 'raisonné *dérèglement* de *tous les sens*' had resulted in a disordering of the mind, which, as if in ironic consolation, he
describes as 'sacré'. In this state, he had envied the 'félicité' of
insects and animals. The contrast between his mental torment
and their mindless bliss is conveyed by the word 'félicité', which
has a deeper meaning than 'bonheur', and normally describes

an inner, spiritual happiness. The irony is intensified by the examples: caterpillars, to represent the innocence of the unbaptised in limbo; and moles, to represent unawakened virginity, 'le sommeil de la virginité' — an ironic echo of his own very different sleep, 'un sommeil dans un nid de flammes', in 'Nuit de l'enfer'. In this embittered state, he had said farewell to the world in 'romances', or ballad-like poems. 'Chanson de la plus haute tour', the poem he quotes next, is a typical example. The theme of impatient longing for an ecstatic happiness links it to the two previous poems; and its thrice-repeated couplet, 'Qu'il vienne, qu'il vienne,/Le temps dont on s'éprenne', is an illustration of the 'refrains niais' and 'rhythmes naïfs' to which reference is made at the beginning of this 'délire'.

As if commenting on the poem, Rimbaud in a prose passage gives examples of his unconventional poetic tastes for the arid, the parched, the faded and the tepid. He then relates how he had, in the stinking alleys of cities, offered himself, like a sacrificial victim, to the sun, imploring the god of fire (apostrophised as 'Général') to attack and destroy the world:

> Bombarde-nous avec des blocs de terre sèche. Aux glaces des magasins splendides! dans les salons! Fais manger sa poussière à la ville. Oxyde les gargouilles. Emplis les boudoirs de poudre de rubis brûlante . . .

Then, in a swift and brilliant transition from the great to the small — from the sun bombarding the earth and its towns to a sunbeam 'dissolving' a gnat in a urinal — he underlines his bitterness by expressing, this time in original anti-aesthetic terms, the envy he felt for the curiously ecstatic, if ephemeral happiness of the lesser animals:

> Oh! le moucheron enivré à la pissotière de l'auberge, amoureux de la bourrache, et que dissout un rayon!

The 'moucheron', appropriately enamoured of the diuretic borage, recalls the 'sales mouches' mentioned in the 'Chanson' and leads to further animal imagery in the second of the next two poems, 'Faim' and 'Le loup criait sous les feuilles'. The first develops the theme of aridity and hardness and evokes in rhythmically stressed simple words, like those of a *comptine* (a child's counting-out rhyme), the poet's virile hunger:

FAIM

Si j'ai du goût, ce n'est guère
Que pour la terre et les pierres.
Je déjeune toujours d'air,
De roc, de charbons, de fer.

Mes faims, tournez. Paissez, faims,
  Le pré des sons.
Attirez le gai venin
  Des liserons.

Mangez les cailloux qu'on brise,
Les vieilles pierres d'églises;
Les galets des vieux déluges,
Pains semés dans les vallées grises.

This frustrated hunger has resulted in an example of what Rimbaud had earlier called 'd'espèces de romances'. It differs, however, from the usual *romance* in being vital and entirely unsentimental. The poet's hunger has impelled him to reject the clichés and stale symbols of generations of writers who had been 'inspired' by nature, and to rediscover her in the harshest as well as in the most ethereal of her features. The concluding stanza, with its thrice-repeated affirmation that stone is the poet's bread, also implies his rejection of traditional religious symbols, such as Christ 'the bread of life'.

'Le loup criait sous les feuilles' continues, once more through animal images (wolf, fowl, spider), the theme of hunger and frustration. In the last stanza, the mocking jingle of rhymes and assonances ('Le bouillon court sur la rouille') surprisingly mingles 'broth' and 'rust' with the idea of death; and the biblical allusions to the altars of Solomon and the brook of Cedron (which Christ crossed on his way to betrayal and crucifixion) again suggest Rimbaud in the role of sacrificial victim:

Que je dorme! que je bouille
Aux autels de Salomon.
Le bouillon court sur la rouille
Et se mêle au Cédron.

The prose passage which makes a transition to the next poem,

'L'Éternité', stresses, on the other hand, purity, gold and life: 'Je vécus étincelle d'or de la lumière *nature*'; and the poem itself, in lyrical yet semi-ironic tones, implies that this fleeting union of the individual with nature could be made universal and eternal. But it also emphasises patience, tenacity, mental anguish, and all that must be endured before we can say:

> Elle est retrouvée!
> — Quoi? — l'éternité.
> C'est la mer mêlée
> Au soleil.

In the last part of 'Délires II', Rimbaud refers to himself as an 'opéra fabuleux', a striking expression which could apply to the world of the *Illuminations*, where he had illustrated the human comedy; but, in the context, it refers to his 'folie' and to his particular kind of imagination, the opposite of empathic. Instead of enabling him to project feelings on to people and external phenomena, his imagination had absorbed everything into his inner life, transforming it and driving him to the confines of the world and to the verge of madness. This was the final and anguished consequence of the statement he had made at the beginning of the section about possessing all possible landscapes within his own mind. Everything was then *in* his mind; and its state resembled the 'tempête sous un crâne' described by Hugo in *Les Misérables*, with its 'chaos des chimères', its 'fournaise des rêves' and its 'pandemonium des sophismes' — an analogy that could be pressed more closely, for Rimbaud may well have considered his *Saison en enfer* to be what Hugo terms 'le poème de la conscience humaine'. At all events, this particular 'délire' is both a storm inside Rimbaud's skull and a coherent poem; and, paradoxically, the climax is expressed in intellectually controlled rhythms, sound patterns and arabesques of magnificent prose:

> Ma santé fut menacée. La terreur venait. Je tombais dans des sommeils de plusieurs jours, et, levé, je continuais les rêves les plus tristes. J'étais mûr pour le trépas, et par une route de dangers ma faiblesse me menait aux confins du monde et de la Cimmérie, patrie de l'ombre et des tourbillons.
> Je dus voyager, distraire les enchantements assemblés sur

mon cerveau. Sur la mer, que j'aimais comme si elle eût dû
me laver d'une souillure, je voyais se lever la croix consolatrice. J'avais été damné par l'arc-en-ciel. Le Bonheur était
ma fatalité, mon remords, mon ver: ma vie serait toujours
trop immense pour être dévouée à la force et à la beauté.

Claudel has written an enthusiastic commentary on the beauty
of the sounds, the rhythms and the melodic line in this 'miracle'
of French prose, selecting for special praise the sentence about
the 'confins du monde', and the sentence ('si grand et si pathé-
tique') about the cross — which ends with the perfect alexandrine: 'je voyais se lever la croix consolatrice'.[5] The appearance
of the cross over the sea, the sea which in 'Le Bateau ivre' had
produced so many visions, is both surprising and ironic. Like
the rainbow, it is a religious symbol, reminding Rimbaud of his
enslavement to his baptism and the beliefs of the Catholic
Church, and therefore powerless to help him. It is the symbol
of his damnation; but the damnation, which before was expressed in terms of Catholic iconography, of the Devil and hell
fire, is now of a less melodramatic but more insidious kind.
It is the inescapable happiness into which every human being
is fated to descend. Happiness is, in fact, the main subject of the
prose passage (the word 'bonheur' occurs three times) and also
of the poem, where it is the theme. This is not, however, the
ecstatic happiness of 'L'Éternité', but the drab happiness of
ordinary mortals, 'une fatalité de bonheur!':

> Ô saisons, ô châteaux!
> Quelle âme est sans défauts?
> J'ai fait la magique étude
> Du bonheur, qu'aucun n'élude.

The poem links Rimbaud's season in hell to the world of our
seasons, where the 'châteaux' (prestigious refuges for alchemists, mystics, mortals — and for the soul) are as transient
as time itself. The question 'Quelle âme est sans défauts?'
is rhetorical. No soul is flawless; and this universal statement
is, in its lyrical simplicity, the most poignant of Rimbaud's
confessions. The final sentences, 'Cela s'est passé. Je sais
aujourd'hui saluer la beauté', are typical of what one might
call Rimbaud's method of resolution through calculated, or

perhaps unconscious, ambiguities. Beauty may be here a eulogistic or a derogatory word (the reference to beauty in the prologue suggests the latter); and 'saluer' can be used to greet and welcome, or to say farewell and dismiss (the draft indicates the second). In fact, the beauty in question is, like the happiness Rimbaud has discussed, a bourgeois value and pursuit; and his conclusion is both contemptuous and definitive.

After the two long and detailed accounts of his 'délires', Rimbaud takes, in 'L'impossible', a broader and a more searching view of himself and of nineteenth-century civilisation. His conflict, although no less intense, now takes place on an abstract, metaphysical plane. The title refers to the impossibility of recapturing various forms of a lost purity: a human purity – the innocence of childhood' a spiritual purity – a pre-Christian state before man's mind had been poisoned by ideas of good and evil; and a philosophic purity – the primitive wisdom of the East. It also suggests the impossibility of finding in the future, either by reason or by faith, any other kind of purity. In a particularly lucid moment, Rimbaud has realised that his deliriums and all his mental aberrations have their source in a corrupt civilisation, which he equates with Christianity. Reason has shown him that everything in his life – childhood, education, religion, behaviour, thoughts, and even dreams, including in particular his dream of evasion and of purity – has been conditioned, and vitiated, by the values of Christian civilisation. His contempt is expressed in an epigrammatic statement, in which the birth of the prototype bourgeois is made to coincide with the birth of Christ: 'M. Prudhomme est né avec le Christ.'[6] But the poet's reason, referred to ironically as 'deux sous de raison', while revealing his own place – and dilemma – in bourgeois society, does not offer a solution; and a characteristic double movement of acceptance followed by rejection of a solution through religion ends the section:

> Ô pureté! pureté!
> C'est cette minute d'éveil qui m'a donné la vision de la
>   pureté!
> – Par l'esprit on va à Dieu!
> Déchirante infortune!

'Déchirante', which describes the 'infortune', also sums up the state of the poet's mind, *torn* between the extremes of a continuing conflict.

'L'Éclair', a section as brief and as explosive as the title, begins with the exclamation, 'Le travail humain!' The idea of work, Rimbaud states, had illuminated from time to time the depths of his hell; and one remembers other occasions such as his cynical references in 'Mauvais sang' to work, science and progress in our 'siècle à mains'. Once more, however, he considers the slogan of the modern world which, with an ironic reversal of the words of the Preacher in the Bible 'All is vanity' (Eccles. 1 : 2), he formulates as: 'Rien n'est vanité; à la science, et en avant!' But this solution is too simple; and, like others he has examined, it has only been proposed in order to be ridiculed and dismissed. Moreover, his impatient, lucid mind sees through these palliatives and distractions (*divertissements*, as Pascal called them) to the inescapable end which they hide from others, namely death. He will therefore continue to protest against the human condition by playing a succession of roles — mountebank, beggar, artist, bandit, and even priest; and at the hour of death, at the risk of losing all hope of eternal salvation, he will launch a desperate attack:

> Non! Non! à présent je me révolte contre la mort! Le travail paraît trop léger à mon orgueil: ma trahison au monde serait un supplice trop court. Au dernier moment, j'attaquerais à droite, à gauche ...
> Alors, — oh! chère pauvre âme, l'éternité serait-elle pas perdue pour nous!

No solution has been found and the conclusion seems a sombre denial of the title. Yet in 'L'Éclair' the forces of childhood and religion, which were pulling Rimbaud back and binding him to the past, have become less potent; and the last sentence where, in 'chère pauvre âme', we hear the cautious voice of the 'Vierge folle', could be read as a defiant challenge rather than as an exclamation of regret.

'Matin' is a pause in the drama and 'aujourd'hui', in the middle of the section, is the pivotal point from which Rimbaud looks back and then forward, as he prepares for the final struggle in 'Adieu':

MATIN

N'eus-je pas *une fois* une jeunesse aimable, héroïque, fabuleuse, à écrire sur des feuilles d'or, — trop de chance! Par quel crime, par quelle erreur, ai-je mérité ma faiblesse actuelle? Vous qui prétendez que des bêtes poussent des sanglots de chagrin, que des malades désespèrent, que des morts rêvent mal, tâchez de raconter ma chute et mon sommeil. Moi, je ne puis pas plus m'expliquer que le mendiant avec ses continuels *Pater* et *Ave Maria*. *Je ne sais plus parler!*

Pourtant, aujourd'hui, je crois avoir fini la relation de mon enfer. C'était bien l'enfer; l'ancien, celui dont le fils de l'homme ouvrit les portes.

Du même désert, à la même nuit, toujours mes yeux las se réveillent à l'étoile d'argent, toujours, sans que s'émeuvent les Rois de la vie, les trois mages, le cœur, l'âme, l'esprit. Quand irons-nous, par delà les grèves et les monts, saluer la naissance du travail nouveau, la sagesse nouvelle, la fuite des tyrans et des démons, la fin de la superstition, adorer — les premiers! — Noël sur la terre!

Le chant des cieux, la marche des peuples! Esclaves, ne maudissons pas la vie.

After 'L'Éclair' and the flashes that have by turns lit up then darkened the hell of the poet's mind, 'Matin' brings light from the outside world, and a sustaining vision. It is the most moving of the nine sections because in it the rhetoric is never gratuitous, but is used to temper and control Rimbaud's agitated emotions, and to give to uniquely personal themes a universal significance. 'Matin' is an unusually poised and harmonious prose poem, and while it appears to be self-contained in its structured symmetry, it is at the same time expansive and resonant with meanings. Closely linked to all that has preceded, it reechoes the prologue, the beginning of the drama, 'Jadis, si je me souviens bien ...' and points to the last act and dénouement in 'Adieu'. It is also related thematically to some of the early poems (one thinks of 'Les Effarés'), to several of the 1872 verse poems (for example,

'Bonne pensée du matin', 'Fêtes de la patience'), and to some of
the *Illuminations* (in particular, 'Jeunesse' and 'Génie').

The title has several meanings. As well as 'the first hours of
the day', and 'morning', it has the figurative sense of 'the
morning of life', and 'jeunesse' – to which Rimbaud refers in
the opening sentence. More important perhaps, and permeating
the text, is the idea of a morning prayer, the first prayer of the
day in the divine service of Matins – but here transposed into
non-religious, anti-Catholic terms. The poem is divided into
two equal parts, at once opposed and complementary. The first,
static and reflective, looks back to the beginning of time, to a
lost paradise; the second looks forward to the new beginning
to which the whole of *Une Saison en enfer* is leading.

Rimbaud begins not with any sign of penitence or gratitude,
nor with a request for help; but, characteristically, with a pro-
testation uttered in a tone of aggrieved indignation. His protest
is ingeniously presented as a rhetorical question, where the
italicised *'une fois'* suggests the possibility of two opposed
meanings: *once* and *never*. The elegant first-person inverted form
of the question, 'N'eus-je pas *une fois* une jeunesse aimable,
héroïque, fabuleuse, . . .', implies, however, a mock-heroic attitude, and a negation, which is made explicit by the sardonic
'trop de chance!'. The sentence is an interesting example of
Rimbaud's use of linguistic contrast between the formal and
the colloquial to give vitality to his narration and a sharper
point to his meaning. Similarly, in the second sentence, the
preciosity of the inversion 'ai-je' is again used in a mocking way,
and with a negating force, to disclaim all personal responsibility
or guilt for his present weakness. He then turns to his audience,
and ironically challenges us, with our 'wisdom', to relate *his*
'chute' – his fall from grace, and his 'sommeil' – the many moments of weariness, physical and mental, to which he has
succumbed during his season in hell; and he states that he himself is no more capable of giving an explanation than the beggar
mouthing everlasting Paternosters and Ave Marias. But this is
a pretence, a rhetorical device, for he knows that the end is in
sight, and that there is now little need for further speech or
narration: 'Pourtant, aujourd'hui, je crois avoir fini la relation
de mon enfer. C'était bien l'enfer; l'ancien, celui dont le fils de
l'homme ouvrit les portes.' The affirmation suggests relief; but

it also implies that his *Saison en enfer*, although as 'real' as the biblical hell, is an 'invention', a work of art which will end when his account of it – his 'relation' – ends. The statement also reflects the belief underlying this poem, and indeed the entire work, that damnation is not eternal, hell is only for a 'season'. It is a personal affair, 'mon enfer', as he says here; a state of mind, 'Je me crois en enfer, donc j'y suis', as he said in 'Nuit de l'enfer'. This belief (or arrogant assumption) of the non-believer is the mainspring of *Une Saison en enfer*.

In the opening of the second part of the poem, the twice repeated 'même' and the twice repeated 'toujours' emphasise the monotony of a vigil which has so far produced mainly frustration and lassitude. But the rhythm has changed and, despite the biblical allusions, the accent is on this earth and this life, on the human as opposed to the divine. The Son of God has become the 'fils de l'homme', and the three wise men are three 'Rois de la vie' – heart, soul and mind. The star shines not for the birth of the Christ child, but for the birth of a new kind of work and a new wisdom, for the end of tyrannies and superstition. Even if the question 'Quand irons-nous . . .' is left unanswered, the movement is towards the future and a new Noël, or 'day of birth', in the original sense of the word, when the song of the heavens will be identified with the progress of humanity. Inspired and sustained by this vision, Rimbaud is able to accept, in common with others, his condition as one of life's 'slaves' – slaves of the work to which our 'chute' (original sin) has condemned us. He ends, as he began, with an equivocal figure of rhetoric, 'Esclaves, ne maudissons pas la vie', a litotes in which 'ne maudissons pas' could be read as 'bénissons'; but the command, although expressing hope, is tinged with reproof and resignation.

In the last section, 'Adieu', the opening words 'L'automne déjà!' convey Rimbaud's startled awakening to the present and to reality; and the theme of the seasons, and more generally of time, announced in the first section and heard repeatedly throughout the work, becomes fully orchestrated. As he had previously played at being others but never himself, so, living in a mythical past, an impossible future, and an imaginary present, he had played with all the fictional devices of time.

Now, in a succession of allusions to the seasons, light, the sun, morning, night, the eve, dawn and 'l'heure nouvelle', he expresses the reality of time's irreversible flow. He can, at last, accept 'real' time because, although it reveals his failure as a *voyant*, it offers hope of a tangible victory, in the life of this world. The autumn may be, as for the Romantic poets, the season of melancholy and nostalgia; but it is also the moment for action and a definitive turning towards the future. Moreover, the idea of autumn brings fresh inspiration, and introduces two singularly appropriate images which dominate the section and are intimately related to many of the main themes —the quest, the town, and *voyance*.

The first image, associated with mists, a city-port, poverty and degradation, is that of a boat, symbol of the journeys through life:

> Notre barque élevée dans les brumes immobiles tourne vers le port de la misère, la cité énorme au ciel taché de feu et de boue.

The second, preceded by an apocalyptic vision reminiscent of 'Matin', is of a golden boat, symbol of the journeys he has made in his imagination since 'Le Bateau ivre':

> Quelquefois je vois au ciel des plages sans fin couvertes de blanches nations en joie. Un grand vaisseau d'or, au-dessus de moi, agite ses pavillons multicolores sous les brises du matin.

These particular images echo and sum up the two 'délires', the 'barque' corresponding to human 'madness'; the 'vaisseau d'or' to literary 'madness', the 'alchimie du verbe', appropriately demonstrated here, as the ship of life is metamorphosed into the ship of beauty. In addition, they reach further back to the very beginning of *Une Saison en enfer*, where Rimbaud had indicated that the stress throughout his work would fall first on life ('ma vie') and then on literature ('la Beauté').

The second image, the golden ship with its many-coloured flags fluttering in the morning breeze, is linked, by references to 'matin' and 'or', to the previous poem, 'Matin'; and its 'pavillons' recall those in the *Illuminations*. Indeed, this unusually potent image represents all that Rimbaud had created or at-

tempted to create; as well as the godlike powers he thought he
had acquired, and which he now renounces:

> J'ai créé toutes les fêtes, tous les triomphes, tous les drames.
> J'ai essayé d'inventer de nouvelles fleurs, de nouveaux astres,
> de nouvelles chairs, de nouvelles langues. J'ai cru acquérir
> des pouvoirs surnaturels. Eh bien! je dois enterrer mon
> imagination et mes souvenirs! Une belle gloire d'artiste et de
> conteur emportée!
>
> Moi! moi qui me suis dit mage ou ange, dispensé de toute
> morale, je suis rendu au sol, avec un devoir à chercher, et la
> réalité rugueuse à étreindre! Paysan!

The poet who had imagined that he was a seer, an angel, a
Promethean stealer of fire and omnipotent, is now forced to
realise that he is no more than a 'Paysan!'

Paradoxically, Rimbaud signals this renunciation of his poetic
ambitions with a remarkable series of images: on his face, 'le
sang séché fume'; behind him stands the 'horrible arbrisseau'
of good and evil; above him, 'un grand vaisseau d'or' and 'des
plages sans fin couvertes de blanches nations en joie'; and in
front and all around him, 'la réalité rugueuse'. This return to
earth from the peaks of ambition is harsh and brutal; and the
identification with the peasant, who embodies what Rimbaud
most despised — manual work, 'la main à charrue' and our
'siècle à mains' — is exceptionally ironical. But 'paysan' can still
mean, as it once did, someone who belongs to a 'pays', who
has a country, a background and a human context. Instead of
provoking a rhetorical outburst of indignation, as one might
have expected, this ironic revelation becomes the occasion for
a display of controlled artistry, and Rimbaud uses the image of
the 'paysan', the last of a series of related images — the convict,
the serf, the mercenary, the outcast, the damned, the negro,
the infernal bridegroom — to obtain effects of repetition,
alliteration and, above all, contrast. For this ignoble creature is
also a heroic figure who grapples with reality and moves onward
with a firm unwavering tread. Hence, if the realisation that he
is a peasant is a defeat, it is also the signal for another departure.
This 'départ' becomes an adieu to the emotions and sensations
he had written about in the *Illuminations*. Henceforth he will
rely on the common virtues of duty, patience, and tenacity.

Disillusioned by the cities and towns of his imagination, he
prepares to enter (and the verb can be taken in its literal sense)
other towns 'splendides villes', which, stripped of the illusions of
literature, shine with the light of their own reality:

> Cependant c'est la veille. Recevons tous les influx de vigueur
> et de tendresse réelle. Et à l'aurore, armés d'une ardente
> patience, nous entrerons aux splendides villes.
>
> Que parlais-je de main amie! Un bel avantage, c'est que je
> puis rire des vieilles amours mensongères, et frapper de
> honte ces couples menteurs, — j'ai vu l'enfer des femmes
> là-bas; —et il me sera loisible de *posséder la vérité dans une*
> *âme et un corps.*

In the *Illuminations* Rimbaud had explored the limits of the
known and the imaginary and, as he declared in 'Enfance', he
had frequently been near to the abyss: 'Ce ne peut être que la
fin du monde en avançant.' Now, however, he has no need of
help or of a 'main amie'. Unaided he will find the truth, not
through poetry, but in himself. The ultimate identification does
indeed seem to be with himself, with the fundamental duality
of body and spirit, which is the source of all the dualities and
conflicting themes in *Une Saison en enfer*. In stressing this concluding statement, he is also stressing the unity underlying the
extraordinary diversity of his personality and his work. But
what is meant by 'posséder la vérité'? What is this truth, and
how can it be possessed? Is Rimbaud thinking of yet another
quest, or does he intend to remain intact and keep, 'avare
comme la mer', what he already possesses? In the previous
sections he has touched upon, highlighted and dramatised
countless emotions, conflicts, clashes of opposites and dualities;
but nothing has been developed or fully explored. The final
declaration is as abstract and general as his other statements —
and it is projected into the future. Everything has been said, but
everything still remains to be done. Since 'Les Déserts de
l'amour', a short earlier prose work, Rimbaud has, however,
transformed his solitude, with its vulnerability as well as its
potential strength, into the semblance of a hard-won victory.
Une Saison en enfer, like most of his work, is both 'closed' and
'open', final and provisional, an end and a beginning.

Une Saison en enfer has ended, as it began, with the emphasis
on the 'je' and the 'moi' —on Rimbaud himself. The plural form

of the pronoun, however, is also used in alternation with the
'je'; and although the 'nous' is often only a rhetorical artifice
to express a personal attitude of irony, disdain, false modesty,
imperiousness or feigned politeness, it refers at times to us, to
mankind. Indeed, Rimbaud shows by the tone he adopts, by the
nature of some of his visions, and by lapidary statements and
wide-ranging generalisations, that he is himself aware that his
work has universal significance. In the last section, as if fully
conscious of this, and of the importance and majesty of his
'Adieu', he begins, for the first time, with 'nous': 'Nous sommes
engagés à la découverte de la clarté divine . . .' And he does not
speak for himself alone when he affirms: 'Recevons tous les
influx de vigueur et de tendresse réelle. Et à l'aurore, armés d'une
ardente patience, nous entrerons aux splendides villes.' His
words voice the age-long hope that man will one day enter into
his full human heritage. The stress finally falls on the one
fundamental duality, that of mind and body — as old as man
himself; and on a quest that is eternal — the quest for truth.

Reference was made at the beginning of this chapter to the
letter of May 1873 in which Rimbaud, feverishly composing the
work that was to become *Une Saison en enfer*, declared: 'Mon sort
dépend de ce livre.' At the time, he may have been thinking
that the book, when finished, would enable him to escape
finally from 'la *mother*' (as he calls her in the same letter), and
from Roche, the 'triste trou' where she had confined him. But,
as the work progressed, he must have realised that his 'fate',
and that of his book, were destined to be more than personal
or local. Everything in the interrelated aspects of its content and
structure, especially the movement between the 'I' and 'others',
between the particular and the general, suggests that he is speaking not only as an individual but also as a representative, or
at least a member, of modern society. We are never allowed to
forget the social context within which he writes, and that
his conflicts spring from its divisions. In his journey of self-
discovery, Rimbaud has touched on, and laid bare, most of the
conflicts, ambivalent emotions, and dualisms that exist in
Western man. Now, at a distance of more than a century,
we can see that, if at one level *Une Saison en enfer* expresses
the crisis in the life of an adolescent struggling for self-fulfilment
in the year 1873, at another level it represents a crisis in our
own materialistic civilisation.

8

LAST POEM AND LAST LETTERS

On 14 October 1875 Rimbaud wrote a letter to Ernest Delahaye which had in it a poem, 'Rêve'. Although this may have been composed earlier, it was copied out and written as part of the letter on that precise date; and it can be said, with little risk of contradiction, that it is the last dated poem of which we have definite knowledge. To appreciate its significance it must be read in the context of the letter:

> (Charleville) 14 Octobre (18)75.
> Reçu le Postcard et la lettre de V. il y a huit jours. Pour tout simplifier, j'ai dit à la Poste d'envoyer ses restantes chez moi, de sorte que tu peux écrire ici, si encore rien aux restantes. Je ne commente pas les dernières grossièretés du Loyola, et je n'ai plus d'activité à me donner de ce côté-là à présent, comme il paraît que la 2° 'portion' du 'contingent' de la 'classe 74' va-t-être appelée le trois novembre suivant ou prochain: la chambrée de nuit:

> RÊVE

> On a faim dans la chambrée —
>   C'est vrai ...
> Émanations, explosions. Un génie:
>   'Je suis le gruère! —
> Lefebvre: 'Keller!'
> Le génie: 'Je suis le Brie! —
> Les soldats coupent sur leur pain:
>   'C'est la vie!
> Le génie. —'Je suis le Roquefort!
>   —'Ça s'ra not' mort! ...
>   —Je suis le gruère
>   Et le Brie! ... etc.

VALSE

On nous a joints, Lefebvre et moi, etc.

De telles préoccupations ne permettent que de s'y absor-
bère. Cependant renvoyer obligeamment, selon les occases,
les 'Loyolas' qui rappliqueraient.

Un petit service : veux-tu me dire précisément et concis —
en quoi consiste le 'bachot' ès sciences actuel, partie
classique, et mathém., etc. — Tu me dirais le point de chaque
partie que l'on doit atteindre : mathém., phys., chim.,
etc., et alors des titres, immédiat, (et le moyen de se procurer)
des livres employés dans ton collège ; par ex. pour ce 'Bachot',
à moins que ça ne change aux diverses universités : en tous
cas, de professeurs ou d'élèves compétents, t'informer à ce
point de vue que je te donne. Je tiens surtout à des choses
précises, comme il s'agirait de l'achat de ces livres pro-
chainement. Instruct. militaire et 'bachot', tu vois, me
feraient deux ou trois agréables saisons ! Au diable d'ailleurs
ce 'gentil labeur'. Seulement sois assez bon pour m'indiquer
le plus mieux possible la façon comment on s'y met.

Ici rien de rien.

J'aime à penser que le Petdeloup et les gluants pleins
d'haricots patriotiques ou non ne te donnent pas plus
de distraction qu'il ne t'en faut. Au moins ça ne schlingue
pas la neige, comme ici.

À toi 'dans la mesure de mes faibles forces'.

Tu écris :

A. Rimbaud.
31, rue Saint-Barthélemy,
Charleville (Ardennes), va sans dire.

P.S. La corresp. en 'passepoil' arrive à ceci que le 'Némery'
avait confié les journaux du Loyola à un *agent de police* pour
me les porter !

The slangy badinage is the style Rimbaud often adopted when
writing to his friends, in particular to Verlaine and Delahaye;
and it is the style, or code, at once literary and anti-literary,
pretentious and self-defensive, of an adolescent. Significantly,
it is absent from all the letters he wrote later when grappling
with 'la réalité rugueuse'. The contemptuous reference at the

beginning is to correspondence from Verlaine, and to the latter's
'grossièretés', meaning no doubt his conversion and his religious
poems – all signs, in Rimbaud's eyes, of abject pusillanimity.
In his poetry he had satirised and rejected Verlaine as the
'pitoyable frère' of 'Vagabonds' and the 'Vierge folle' of *Une
Saison en enfer*; but the rejection of the person he now terms
the 'Loyola' is a definitive and real gesture. He did not answer
Verlaine's letter and he never saw him again.

This is one of a series of gestures which express both a turning
away from literature and from the past; and an equally compel-
ling movement towards practical concerns and the future. Some
two years earlier, in a letter dated May 1873 to Delahaye,
Rimbaud had expressed interest in translations of Shakespeare,
and in Goethe's *Faust*, which he asked his friend to send him.
Now he asks him for information about the science *baccalauréat*,
the syllabus, prescribed texts and the standard required; and,
as he was just twenty-one years old, and expecting to be con-
scripted before the end of 1875, his enquiry also includes
military instruction. These new activities will, he adds, keep
him occupied for a few pleasant 'saisons' – a word that recalls
his previous imaginary 'saison' in hell. As regards the call-up,
there should have been no cause for anxiety; as according to a
French law then in force, Rimbaud was, by virtue of his elder
brother Frédéric's five years with the army, exempt from military service; yet the fear of conscription obsessed him all his
life. Years later, when working at Harar, he was still seeking
reassurance that he was not contravening the law; and even in
1891 in hospital, after his right leg had been amputated, he was
haunted by the threat of military service. He wrote to his sister,

> Quelle nouvelle horreur me racontez-vous? Quelle est en-
> core cette histoire de service militaire? . . .

and again

> Enfin, c'est peut-être mon destin de devenir *cul-de-jatte*! À ce
> moment, je suppose que l'administration militaire me
> laisserait tranquille!

and he declared with bitter resignation,

> l'administration militaire est capable d'emprisonner un
> estropié, ne fût-ce que dans un hôpital.

In the letter to Delahaye, however, he is able to dramatise and burlesque as a dream his concern for what he imagines, or fears, will happen in the army and the barrack-room.

'Rêve' is the parody of a Romantic dream — in fact, a nightmare — and the parodic impression is reinforced by the use of literary devices, such as rhymes and assonance, a witty play on words, and by the waltz at the end. But this anti-poem recalls not only other parodies in Rimbaud's work — for instance, those of the *Album zutique* (1871–2) — but also more serious poems like 'Le Cœur volé' and 'Démocratie'. It could indeed be said that 'Rêve' recalls *all* Rimbaud's poems, for it is a parody both of his own poetry and of literature in general, a 'testament', as André Breton saw, but a mocking testament, in which Rimbaud finally rejects his human and literary ambitions. In it he seeks, through derision and burlesque, to escape from or to extinguish the poetic hunger he had once satisfied in dreams and visions.

In 'Rêve' everything is localised, topical and banal. The unexpected references to cheese — 'gruyère' (pronounced 'gruère' in the Ardennes), 'brie' and 'roquefort' — recall other texts on cheeses, such as Saint-Amant's 'Le Fromage', Raoul Ponchon's 'La Question du fromage', and Zola's 'symphonie des fromages' in *Le Ventre de Paris*. But in Rimbaud's poem, cheese and bread replace the 'pré des sons' and the 'bouts d'air noir' of 'Fêtes de la faim'; and emanations and explosions of the human body, and of war, drown the melodious 'rugissement' of the volcanoes in 'Villes'. This is a world of ordinary people, soldiers, and contemporary figures, like Keller, the *député* who advocated three years' compulsory service for all Frenchmen, and the twice-mentioned Lefebvre, son of the owner of a house in Charleville where the Rimbaud family had lived. The conclusion reads like a caricature of the graceful *ariettes* of Favart (whose poetry had influenced both Verlaine and Rimbaud) ending, like some of them, with an invitation to dance. But here the 'Valse' is a perverse dance of human fraternity, the *danse macabre* of war. In this, his last poem, Rimbaud is not merely playing, at various levels, on the sound and the meaning of words, notably, 'guère', 'gruyère', 'guerre'; 'Keller' (a man's name and a cellar); 'génie' (the Engineers and poetic genius); he is playing with the theme of life and death — life in its crudest and most sordid aspect, death in its most 'democratic' and absurd form, 'la vie française, le sentier de l'honneur', as he had described it in *Une Saison en enfer*.

The Surrealists paid special attention to 'Rêve' and gave it, as many critics think, undeserved and excessive praise. For Éluard, it was an example of 'poésie indispensable', and he placed it in the section 'Poésie pure' of *Donner à voir*, calling it 'cet admirable poème de Rimbaud';[1] Breton included it in his *Anthologie de l'humour noir* and said of it: '"Rêve", absolute triumph of pantheistic frenzy, in which the marvellous unites freely with the commonplace and which endures as quintessential as the most mysterious scenes in plays of the Elizabethan period and of the second Faust'.[2] The tone is over-solemn and the praise uncritical, but it is a generous salute to the *voyant*'s final look at literature and 'la vieillerie poétique'.

The letter of 14 October 1875 is important not only because it contains this last poem, but also because it was written at the most decisive of the many turning-points in Rimbaud's career. It marks a dividing line between those letters, mainly of a literary nature, which he had written to friends and fellow poets, and the letters he wrote in Abyssinia to traders, engineers and explorers, and to the once-despised family in Charleville. In a more general sense, it is a watershed between two worlds, West and East; between two ways of life, that of the poet and *voyant* and that of the 'aventurier' and the merchant.

The letters Rimbaud wrote in the remaining sixteen years of his life occupy almost half of the recent Pléiade edition of his works (1972). This correspondence can be divided into two sections: letters written between the end of 1875 and 1880, when he travelled and found occasional employment, mainly in Europe; and those written after 1880 from Aden and Abyssinia, where he worked until his death in 1891. The first period of five years was one of sporadic work and intensive travel to places as diverse as Vienna, Java, Bremen, Sweden, Norway, Alexandria and Cyprus. These wanderings were punctuated by returns to his native Ardennes, and it was during one of these in 1879 that Delahaye asked him if he was still composing poems, and received the scornful reply, 'Je ne m'occupe plus de ça.' After he left Charleville in March 1880, he went to Alexandria and then to Cyprus, from where he made his way to the 'rivages incandescents' of the Red Sea. He finally

reached Aden on 7 August, where he obtained a situation with
the firm of Mazeran, Viannay, Bardey and Company, dealers
in coffee and skins, and was employed by them there and at
their branch office in Harar.

Verlaine aptly called Rimbaud 'l'homme aux semelles de
vent'; but Delahaye emphasised the opposite aspect, 'il eut
toute sa vie des désirs de retour — vers quoi? — vers tout'. These
extremes had been expressed in the poetry through the symbols
of the 'Bateau ivre' and the motionless boat of 'Mémoire'; and in
laconic statements, 'Au revoir ici, n'importe où' ('Démocratie')
and 'On ne part pas. Reprenons les chemins d'ici' ('Mauvais
sang'). Now, they become nothing more than restlessness and
prosaic activity. Only one letter, dated 17 November 1878, to
his mother and sister, describing his arduous crossing of the
St Gotthard, retains the adolescent's keenness of observation,
unclouded by bitterness or self-concern:

> La route, qui n'a guère que six mètres de largeur, est com-
> blée tout le long à droite par une chute de neige de près de
> deux mètres de hauteur, qui, à chaque instant, allonge sur
> la route une barre d'un mètre qu'il faut fendre sous une
> atroce tourmente de grésil. Voici! plus une ombre dessus,
> dessous ni autour, quoique nous soyons entourées d'objets
> énormes; plus de route, de précipices, de gorge ni de ciel:
> rien que du blanc à songer, à toucher, à voir ou ne pas voir...

The letters belonging to the second period are the only evidence we have of Rimbaud's need to continue writing and to
communicate. About a hundred of these were to his 'chers amis',
his mother and his sister Isabelle, and the majority of the
others to his business associates, the most important being
those to Alfred Ilg, a Swiss engineer. This correspondence is in
no sense that of an *homme de lettres*, still less of a poet, and their
place in a study of Rimbaud's literary work may be debatable,
as indeed many writers and critics think. The Surrealists, who
had found in the letter of 14 October 1875 inexplicable but
exalting evidence of a last visitation by the spirit of poetry,
were unable to discover any kind of exaltation, or even interest,
in the subsequent letters. They felt that the eye of the *voyant*
had become the 'regard presque éteint' of the 'aventurier', and
that this Rimbaud was an 'assez lamentable polichinelle' ob-

sessed by practical concerns and above all money. Henri Michaux is even more scornful: 'When I think that there are two or three idiots who imagine they have reconstructed Rimbaud's life from his correspondence! As if letters to his sister, his mother, a schoolmaster, or a pal would yield anything at all.'[3] Other writers have searched the arid tracts of the letters for any suggestion that Rimbaud might still be interested in poetry; and one twentieth-century poet, Jacques Réda, has found what he calls a 'lyrisme objectif' in the inventory of a caravan-load of rifles and percussion-caps for King Menelik of Abyssinia:[4]

1.440 fusils à Th. 7	10.080
300.000 capsules à Th. 1 le mille	300
450.000 capsules à Th. 2 le mille	900
Outils et fournitures en bloc	2.720

If there is any 'lyricism' in the letters, it is not in those to fellow merchants about ammunition, coffee, skins, ivory, haberdashery and saucepans, but in the letters to his mother and sister, in one of which he says, 'si je me plains, c'est une espèce de façon de chanter'. It can be found again in the last, unfinished letter addressed to the 'Directeur des Messageries Maritimes' and dictated to his sister Isabelle on the eve of his death:

UN LOT: UNE DENT SEULE.

UN LOT: DEUX DENTS.

UN LOT: TROIS DENTS.

UN LOT: QUATRE DENTS.

UN LOT: DEUX DENTS.

Monsieur le Directeur,

Je viens vous demander si je n'ai rien laissé à votre compte. Je désire changer aujourd'hui de ce service-ci, dont je ne connais même pas le nom, mais en tout cas que ce soit le service d'Aphinar. Tous ces services sont là partout, et moi, impotent, malheureux, je ne peux rien trouver, le premier chien dans la rue vous dira cela.

Envoyez-moi donc le prix des services d'Aphinar à Suez. Je suis complètement paralysé: donc je désire me trouver de bonne heure à bord. Dites-moi à quelle heure je dois être transporté à bord...

This letter is usually dismissed as 'incoherent', but it is more moving than the last poem. The baffling references to teeth and to lots seem like a distant echo of 'Solde', and the pathetic appeal to be taken on board ship ready for yet another journey continues the theme that dominates his life. André Breton's description of 'Rêve' as Rimbaud's 'testament poétique et spirituel' could more appropriately be applied to this final, tragic letter.

'Lyricism' in the strict meaning of the term does not exist in any of these letters. The *voyant* who had been prepared to sacrifice everything to discover fresh visions is now content with a camera so that he can send to his mother 'des vues du pays et des gens', and of himself, 'ci-inclus deux photographies de moi-même, par moi-même'. He can still dream of unexplored countries, and of journeying into 'l'inconnu'; but he now sees only 'des déserts peuplés de nègres stupides'. Gold, which in his poetry had been the symbol of his verbal alchemy, has now become the measure of worldly success and a perpetual burden: 'Figurez-vous que je porte continuellement dans ma ceinture seize mille et quelques cents francs d'or; ça pèse une huitaine de kilos et ça me flanque la dysenterie', he writes. He is still eager to publish; but his contributions are now for *Le Temps, Le Figaro* and *Le Bosphore Égyptien*; a report of his Greek employee Sotiro's expedition into the Ogaden for the *Comptes rendus des séances de la Société de Géographie*; and — ultimate concession to the bourgeois public — 'quelques récits intéressants' for the *Courrier des Ardennes* about his own travels.

Example after example could be adduced to show that the letters are the obverse, or the inverted image, of the poetry. The quest and the striving for self-fulfilment continue, but the means and the values have changed. His aim, *'posséder la vérité dans une âme et un corps'*, is now to be achieved by conforming in every respect to bourgeois ideas about knowledge, success, marriage and money. His values and his changed attitude to the mother he once called 'la bouche d'ombre' are summed up in a letter from Aden of 8 December 1882 to his 'chère maman': 'Au lieu donc de te fâcher, tu n'as qu'à te réjouir avec moi. Je sais le prix de l'argent . . .' In other letters, the theme is similar, and he writes of his wish to settle down as a *rentier*, to marry and have a son who, equipped with sound practical knowledge, would become a famous engineer, 'un homme puissant et riche par la science'.

Although the years in Abyssinia might be seen as Rimbaud's ultimate rejection of western civilisation, the letters written from there read like a capitulation to its values, against which he had previously directed the whole weight of his genius. At a deeper level they can be seen as a gesture of reparation to his mother, the inflexible embodiment of middle-class virtues. Incapable of understanding poetry, or her son's inner life, she could appreciate the importance of hard work and the value of money. She could accept completely the 'second Rimbaud'. But this is no ordinary atonement and it is far from the stereotype case of the young rebel who in his maturity conforms to the adult's 'wisdom'. Rimbaud, having abandoned his poetic ideals, had pursued his practical ambitions with the same ferocious intensity, and pushed them, and himself, to the extreme limit of endurance, until it seemed that nothing remained except tenacity and frustrated aspiration. At the end of a letter to Isabelle he wrote:

> Voilà le beau résultat: je suis assis, et de temps en temps, je me lève et sautille une centaine de pas sur mes béquilles, et je me rassois. Mes mains ne peuvent rien tenir. Je ne puis, en marchant, détourner la tête de mon seul pied et du bout des béquilles. La tête et les épaules s'inclinent en avant, et vous bombez comme un bossu. Vous tremblez à voir les objets et les gens se mouvoir autour de vous, crainte qu'on ne vous renverse, pour vous casser la seconde patte. On ricane à vous voir sautiller. Rassis, vous avez les mains énervées et l'aisselle sciée, et la figure d'un idiot. Le désespoir vous reprend et vous restez assis comme un impotent complet, pleurnichant et attendant la nuit, qui rapporte l'insomnie perpétuelle et la matinée encore plus triste que la veille, etc., etc. La suite au prochain numéro.

That 'beau résultat' was the end of Rimbaud's quest; yet this 'impotent complet' could still say 'la suite au prochain numéro'.

Even if the letters contain no original ideas, no sense of wonder, no sign of human development —nothing to compensate for the burnt-out poetic genius —their very emptiness, their spiritual vacuum, and the portrait they give of a mutilated human being, are a final, if unconscious comment on the values of our civilisation.

9

CONCLUSION

It is possible to see Rimbaud as the last and most audacious of the Romantic poets, in that he pushed to an extreme conclusion a belief in the poet as prophet, seer, magus or *voyant* – a privileged person endowed with special, if not divine powers. But with the realisation that this belief was a myth and a delusion, he drove himself with no less intensity to the opposite extreme in order to expose and destroy it; and in doing so, destroyed himself. His striving for an absolute, or a perfect state, in which all dualities would be transcended or reconciled, ended in divisions, and the tragic separation of imagination and reality. This fundamental paradox, or logical consequence, can be fully understood only if it is seen (as has been attempted in this study) in the context of an anticlimax: the long descent from the *Illuminations* to the last letters, from the belief in *voyance* to the obstinate but fruitless search for '*la vérité dans une âme et un corps*'.

The paradoxical result has been expressed in epigrammatic form by Benjamin Fondane: 'Everyone *has found*, thanks to Rimbaud. But, strange paradox, he alone seems to have found nothing.'[1] What Rimbaud found, apart from eternal moments of lyricism in his poetry and, in the second part of his life, hardship and frustration, cannot be known. According to his sister Isabelle he received the sacraments just before he died, prayed, and *believed*. Her statement is suspect; but what is certain is that others have, through Rimbaud, found a faith or a belief, while many more have found inspiration in his work.[2] For Fondane, Rimbaud's supreme importance was to have revealed (strange paradox again) the nothingness – the metaphysical absurdity – of our existence. Claudel, on the other hand, found, as he repeatedly stressed, everything in Rimbaud, and it was through a reading of the *Illuminations* and *Une Saison en enfer* that he was led back to the Catholic faith. Mallarmé saw in Rimbaud's life an adventure that was 'unique in the history of

art', while for Valéry he was a 'creator of values' —literary and
mental rather than spiritual — and he placed him, with Mallarmé
and Verlaine, as one of the three 'Rois Mages' of modern poetry.
André Breton revered him as a 'veritable god of adolescence'
and found in his work, particularly the *Illuminations*, a constant
source of exaltation. Camus declared that he was the greatest
of the poets of revolt; René Char acclaimed him as the first poet
of a civilisation not yet born; and French students, during the
événements of 1968, reiterated his aim: 'changer la vie'.

Although taken out of its context and used as an ephemeral
slogan, 'changer la vie' does put the stress where Rimbaud
himself invariably put it. His poetry is more than a series of
'textes' or 'tranches d'écriture'. From the first 'exercises' to the
last anti-poem it has a meaning, as does the misguided struggle
for fulfilment through action, in 'life'. Everything he wrote and
did is a challenge to indifference, complacency, and accepted
values; but his life and work no longer provoke, as they once
did, extreme reactions. This is partly the result of a changed
literary climate (itself the result of social changes) in which
critics are preoccupied with literature as a non-expressive
system of signs, a highly intellectual game, with no assessments
or value-judgements at stake. But the challenge remains as
sharp and as insistent as ever, and it is significant that a recent
questionnaire involving thirty-one writers of various nationali-
ties had the title *aujourd'hui, Rimbaud*.

What Rimbaud himself finally found may have been nothing;
but what he left is inexhaustible. He pioneered the way, and set
an example for the Surrealists' exploration of the unconscious,
making available for them and their successors new subjects and
new images; he was the first to use many of the devices and techniques — especially those needed to give an appropriate form to
the *poème en prose* —which contemporary poets are still developing; and he revitalised and gave a tragic dimension to the themes
of childhood, adolescence, and the wonder and fragility of
human aspirations. His work lacks certain qualities, notably
compassion and maturity, qualities that are part of the genius of
Baudelaire, the first and greatest of the *voyants*; it is less formally
perfect than that of Mallarmé or Valéry, who belong to another
line of poets, the *artistes*; and, compared with the impressively
substantial work of Claudel, Saint-John Perse, or Jouve, it is

slight and fragmented. But Rimbaud stands outside purely literary lines and categories, unique in his unrivalled qualities: a tone of perpetual challenge, a dynamic intensity, and a quickening, visionary power.

TRANSLATED PASSAGES

1   Let the reader now admire, as he should, the poet: never for-
getting, as he reads these pages, that the work, brilliant as it is, comes
from a brain whose real age is only fifteen, sixteen, seventeen or
eighteen.

4—5   Why, I said to myself, learn Greek or Latin? I don't know. In fact
they are useless! What difference does it make to me if I pass the
exam, what use is it if I pass? None, surely. And yet I gather you
get a job only if you pass. But *I* don't want a job, I'll live on a private
income. And even if you did want one, why learn Latin? Nobody
speaks it . . .
    Why learn both history and geography? . . .
    What difference does it make to me if Alexander was famous?
What difference does it make . . . How do we know the Latins ever
existed? Perhaps it's some made-up language; and even if they did
exist, they can let me live on my income and keep their language
for themselves! What harm have I ever done them to be put through
agonies like this?
    And what about Greek? No-one speaks the filthy language, no-one
in the whole wide world! . . . Ah! blithering blather and hell's bells!
I'm going to live on my income; it's not much fun wearing your
trousers out on school benches . . . blithering blathering bells!

                                                            R.L.

5   Your heart has understood: — these children are motherless. No
mother in the home! — and the father is far away! . . .

6   Then, with his great hand splendid in its filth, though the pot-bellied
king sweated, the Blacksmith, a terrifying figure, flung the red cap of
revolution in his face!

7—8   TO MUSIC

                                             Station Square, Charleville

Around the square cut up into paltry lawns, with its prim trees and
flowers in the garden, all the wheezy well-to-do, stifled by the heat
of a Thursday evening, ponderously parade their stupid jealousies.
The military bandsmen in the middle of the garden nod their shakos

to the *Fifers' Waltz*; around them, in the front rows, struts a fop; and a notary hangs from his watch-chain with its seals and trinkets. Monocled landlords emphasise all the wrong notes: these great bloated bureaucrats trail their fat wives flanked by an officious posse of attendants like elephant-handlers in flounces of self-advertisement; on the green benches, clubs of retired grocers poke the sand with their pommelled sticks and discuss the treaties in serious tones, then they take pinches of snuff from silver boxes and continue: 'All in all . . .'. Spreading his buxom buttocks on a bench, a bourgeois with pale buttons holding in his Flemish belly relishes his quality pipe overflowing with strands of tobacco — contraband of course; ragamuffins go sniggering all along the green lawns; and, their thoughts turned to love by the schmalz of the trombones, wide-eyed and smoking pinks, soldiers chuck babies under their chins to lead their nannies on . . .

As for me, dishevelled like a student, I follow the pert little girls under green chestnut-trees: they know my game, and turn towards me laughing, their eyes full of indiscretions. I say not a word: I simply stare at the flesh on their white necks criss-crossed with unruly curls: I follow, beneath their bodices and flimsy clothes, the heavenly line of their backs down from the curve of their shoulders. Soon I've undone a shoe, a stocking . . . In a fine fever, I reconstruct their bodies. They find me funny and whisper to each other . . . And my brutal desires clutch at their lips . . .

R.L.

10   Sweet as the Lord of the cedar and of hyssops, I piss towards the dark skies, very high and very far, with the approval of the tall heliotropes.

14   If brass awakens as a trumpet, it's in no way to blame. To me that's obvious: I am present at the birth of my thought: I look at it, I listen to it: I make a sweep with the bow: the symphony stirs in the depths, or comes with a leap on to the stage.

14—15   The Poet makes himself into a *visionary* by a long, immense and reasoned *disordering* of *all the senses*. All forms of love, of suffering, of madness; he himself seeks and consumes within himself all poisons, so as to keep only their quintessences. Unspeakable torture in which he needs all his faith, all superhuman strength, in which he becomes above all others the great sufferer, the great criminal, the great accursed, — and the supreme Scholar! — For he reaches the *unknown!* Because he has cultivated his soul, already rich, more than anyone else! He reaches the unknown, and if, driven mad, he should end by losing the meaning of his visions, he has seen them! Let him die as he surges through unheard-of and unnameable things: other dread workers will come; they will begin at the horizons where he collapsed!

18 THE STOLEN HEART

My sad heart's foaming at the poop,
My heart with cheap tobacco strewn:
On it they hurl their spurts of soup;
My sad heart's foaming at the poop:
Under the taunting of the troop
Which choruses a laugh in tune,
My sad heart's foaming at the poop,
My heart with cheap tobacco strewn.

Hard from the tommy's ribald realm
Their taunts have left my heart depraved!
Pictures pinned up beside the helm
Come from the tommy's ribald realm.
O let the magic sea o'erwhelm
My heart with purifying waves!
Hard from the tommy's ribald realm
Their taunts have left my heart depraved!

After their quids have lost their juice
What shall we do, my stolen heart?
Bacchic hiccups will be loosed
After their quids have lost their juice:
And if my heart has been abused
My poor insides will give a start:
After their quids have lost their juice,
What shall we do, my stolen heart?

R.L.

19—20 *To Mr P. Demeny*

POETS AGED SEVEN

And Mother, closing the homework book, went off satisfied and very
proud, without seeing, in his blue eyes and under his beetling brow,
the soul of her child invested with repugnance.

All day he sweated with obedience; highly intelligent; yet dark
traits, a few tics, seemed to suggest for sure bitter hypocrisies
in him. In the shade of corridors with their musty hangings, he
went by and stuck out his tongue, thrusting his fists into his
groin and seeing spots before his closed eyes. A door would open
on to the evening: by the lamplight he could be seen up there
against the banisters, raging, in a pit of daylight hanging down from
the roof. In summer especially, vanquished, stupid, he insisted on
shutting himself in the cool of the latrines: there he used to think,
quietly, relishing his nostrils. When, washed of day's smells, the
garden-patch behind the house, in winter, caught the moonlight,
lying at the foot of a wall, buried in the marl and squashing his
giddy eye to see visions, he listened to the tainted espaliers swarm-
ing. Have pity! His only friends were those sickly children who,

with bare heads, the colour of the eyes fading on to their cheeks, and hiding their thin fingers, yellow and black with mud, under clothes stinking of diarrhoea, all in rags, talked with the gentleness of idiots! And if his mother caught him at foul friendships, she took fright; the child's profound tenderness launched itself at this astonishment. It was good. She had blue eyes — which lie!

At the age of seven, he used to imagine novels, on life in the open desert, where ravished Liberty shines forth, forests, suns, shores, savannas! — He made use of illustrated magazines in which he blushed to see the laughter of Spanish and Italian girls. When the crazy brown-eyed daughter of the workers next door came round — aged eight — dressed in printed calico, the little brute, and had jumped on his back in a corner, shaking her locks, he bit her buttocks when he was underneath her, for she never wore drawers; and, bruised by her fists and heels, he carried the smells of her skin back to his room.

He used to dread the colourless December Sundays when, perched on a small mahogany table, his hair well oiled, he read from a Bible with a cabbage-green edge to its leaves; dreams oppressed him every night in his recess. He did not love God; but the men, black, in overalls, whom he saw returning on tawny evenings to the suburb where town-criers, with three rolls on their drums, make the crowd laugh or grumble at the announcements. He would dream of the love-making meadow where luminous swells, healthy smells, and golden pubescences move about calmly and take their flight!

And how he most enjoyed sombre things, when, in the bare bedroom, high-ceilinged and blue behind its closed shutters, reeking of acrid damp, he read his unceasingly pondered novel, full of heavy ochre skies and drowned forests, of flowers of flesh open wide on the sidereal woods, vertigo, collapses, routs and pity! — while the background noise of his part of town went on below — alone, and lying on lengths of unbleached canvas, with violent presentiments of sailcloth.

R.L.

22   Above all, put into rhyme an account of the potato blight!

24   VOWELS

A black, E white, I red, U green, O blue: vowels, one day I shall tell of your latent births: A, the hairy black waistcoat of detonating flies buzzing around ferocious smells, gulfs of shadow; E, the whiteness of mists and tents, the lances of lofty glaciers, white kings, the quiver of umbels; I, crimson, blood spat out, the laughter of beautiful lips in anger or the intoxication of repentance; U, cycles, the divine vibration of verdant seas, the peace of pastures sprinkled with animals, the peace of furrows imprinted by alchemy on broad, studious brows; O, the supreme Trumpet full of strange stridencies, silences

traversed by Worlds and Angels: O for Omega, the purple light from
His Eyes!

R.L.

25   This language will be of the soul for the soul, summing up everything,
scents, sounds, colours, thought grappling on to thought and pulling.

27   I invented the colour of the vowels! — *A* black, *E* white, *I* red, *O* blue,
U green. — I regulated the form and the movement of each consonant,
and, with instinctive rhythms, I prided myself on inventing a poetic
language accessible, some day, to all the senses.

27   The star has wept pink in the heart of your ears, infinity flowed white
from your neck to your loins; the sea has rolled russet on your ver-
milion breasts and Man bled black at your sovereign womb.

R.L.

29   Pour us your poison to comfort us! This fire so burns our minds
that we want to plunge to the bottom of the abyss, Hell or Heaven,
what does it matter? To the bottom of the Unknown to find something *new*!

30   I know the skies bursting with lightning, and the waterspouts, under-
tow and currents: I know the evening, Dawn exalted like a nation
of doves, and at times I have seen what men believe they have seen!
I have seen the setting sun, spotted with mystical horrors, casting
its slow-clotting violet light, like actors in ancient dramas, on the
waves shuddering in the distance like shutters! I have dreamed of
green night with dazzled snows, a kiss rising slowly to the seas'
eyes, of the flow of unimagined sap, and of the yellow and blue
awakening of singing phosphorus! I have followed for months on
end the swell storming reefs like hysterical cattle, without imagining
that the glowing feet of the Maries could wrench the wheezing
Ocean round by the muzzle! I have crashed, you know, into incre-
dible Floridas, where flowers are mixed with the eyes of panthers
sporting the skins of men! Rainbows as taut as bridles under the
seas' horizon, with glaucous herds! I have seen enormous marshes
fermenting, sargassos where a whole Leviathan rotted among the
rushes! Water collapsing amid halcyon calm, and distances cascad-
ing towards abysses!

31   I who trembled as I felt the whine, fifty miles away, of rutting Behe-
moths and dense Maelstroms, travelling eternally across blue immo-
bilities, I miss Europe with its ancient parapets! I have seen starry
archipelagos! and islands whose delirious skies are open to the
drifter: — Is it in those unfathomable nights that you sleep and go
into exile, O future Vigour, you million golden birds? True, I have
wept too much, though! The Dawns are heart-rending. Every moon
is atrocious and every sun is bitter: acrid love has distended me with
intoxicating torpors. O let my keel burst open! O let me go to the sea!

If I long for European water, it is for the cold, black puddle where, towards balmy nightfall, a child, crouching in utter sadness, launches a boat as frail as a butterfly in May. No longer can I, bathed in your languishings, O waves, take the wake from the cotton-carriers, nor cross the pride of flags and pennants, nor swim under the horrible gaze of pontoons.

R.L.

37   Immense Dreams or Journeys, through nights of Truth . . .

39   What flocks of birds! o iaio, iaio! . . .
      — La Juliette, that recalls l'Henriette,

39   Appreciate this turn, so gay, so easy: it is mere waves, flowers, and it is your family!

      Then it sings. O so gay, so easy, and visible to the naked eye . . . — I sing with it, —

      Appreciate this turn, so gay, so easy: it is mere waves, flowers, and it is your family!

R.L.

40   To you, Nature, I give myself; with my hunger and all my thirst.

40   It is found again. What? — Eternity. It's the sea gone with the sun.

41   There were black countries, lakes, poles, colonnades under the blue night, railway stations.
      The wind, from the sky, threw icicles on to the ponds.

42–3   MEMORY

I

Clear water; like salt from children's tears, the assault in the sun of the brilliance of women's bodies; the silk, a mass of lily white, of banners besieging walls defended by a maid; the frolic of angels; — No . . . the golden current flowing forwards moves its black, and heavy, and ever so cool arms of grass. She, darkling, with the blue Heavens for a canopy over her bed, summons for curtains the shadows of hill and arch.

II

O! the wet pane proffers its limpid bubbles! Water drapes the waiting beds in pale, unfathomable gold. The little girls' faded green dresses act as willow-trees for the acrobatics of unbridled birds. Purer than a sovereign, a warm yellow eyelid, the marsh marigold — O Wife, thy marriage vows! — promptly at noon, from its dull mirror, envies in the sky grey with heat the pink and well-loved Sphere.

III

The lady stands too upright in the next meadow where the gossamer of handiwork snows down; her parasol held in her fingers, she treads on umbels, too lordly a lady; children read their red morocco book in the flower-strewn pasture! Alas, He, like a thousand white angels who part on the road, journeys beyond the mountain! She, quite cold, and black, runs! after the man's departure.

IV

Sadness of thick young arms of pure grass! The gold of April moons at the heart of the holy bed! Joy of riverside work-yards left to themselves, a prey to August evenings which make rottenness flourish! Let her weep now beneath the ramparts! the breath of the poplars up there is the only breeze. Then comes the still water, without reflections, without a spring, grey: an old man, dredging, toils in his motionless boat.

V

A plaything of this wretched patch of water, I cannot — O motionless boat! O arms too short! — pick either flower: neither the yellow one which annoys me, here; nor the blue one, at home in the ash-coloured water. Ah! the flutter of dust from willows shaken by a wing! The reed-roses long since devoured! My boat still immobile; and its chain drawn towards the depths of the limitless lake — to what mud?

R.L.

47   Idle youth, a slave to everything, through delicacy have I wasted my life. Ah! may the time come when hearts fall in love!

R.L.

52–3   AFTER THE FLOOD

As soon as the idea of the Flood had settled down, a hare stopped among the sainfoin and the nodding bells and said his prayer to the rainbow through a spider's web. O the precious stones which hid themselves — the flowers which stared already!

In the dirty main street butchers' stalls went up, and boats were hauled towards the sea rising in tiers as it does in engravings. Blood flowed, at Bluebeard's — in slaughterhouses — in circuses, where the sign of God showed wanly at the windows. Blood and milk flowed. Beavers built. Laced coffee steamed in the estaminets. In the great house of glass, still streaming, children in mourning looked at the wonderful pictures.

A door slammed — and on the village square a child twirled his arms, understood by weathervanes and steeple cocks everywhere,

in the dazzling shower. Madame*** set up a piano in the Alps.
Mass and first communions were celebrated at the hundred thous-
and altars in the cathedral. Caravans set off. And the Hotel Splendide
was built in the chaos of ice and night at the pole.

Since then, the Moon heard the jackals howling across deserts
of thyme — and georgics in clogs grumbling in the orchard. Then,
in the purple coppice, burgeoning, Eucharis told me it was spring.
Rise, lake — Foam, roll over the bridge and the woods; — black
shrouds and organs — thunder and lightning — rise and roll on;
Water and sadness, rise and revive the Floods. For since they have
subsided — O the precious stones hiding themselves, and the
flowers open wide! — it's sheer tedium! and the Queen, the Witch
who lights her embers in the earthen pot, will never want to tell us
what she knows and we do not.

R.L.

56   CHILDHOOD

                                III

In the wood there is a bird, its song makes you stop and blush.
There is a clock that does not strike.
There is a mire with a nest of white creatures.
There is a cathedral that goes down and a lake that comes up.
There is a little carriage abandoned in the copse, or which goes
    running down the path, its ribbons streaming.
There is a troupe of little actors in costume, glimpsed on the road
    through the edge of the wood.
There is, to end with, when you are hungry and thirsty, someone
    chasing you away.

R.L.

60   FLOWERS

From a golden dais — among silken cords, grey gauze, green velvet
and crystal discs which darken like bronze in the sun — I can see
the foxglove open on a carpet of silver filigree, eyes and hair.

Golden yellow coins strewn on agate, mahogany pillars supporting a dome made of emeralds, gathers of white satin and fine ruby
rods surround the water-rose.

Like a god with huge blue eyes and shaped like snow, sea and sky
attract to marble terraces a crowd of young and vigorous roses.

R.L.

64   TOWN

I am an ephemeral and not too discontented citizen of a metropolis
considered modern because any known taste has been avoided in
the furnishing and facing of the houses as well as in the plan of the
town. Here you will find no trace of any monument to superstition.
Morality and language are reduced to their simplest expression at
last! These millions of people who do not need to know one another

treat education, a job and old age so alike that this kind of life must be several times shorter than what some crazy statistic givers for people on the continent. So, from my window, I see new ghosts rolling through the thick and eternal coal-smoke — our shadowy wood, our midsummer night! — new Fates, in front of my cottage which is my homeland and all my heart since everything here resembles this — Death dry-eyed, our busy servant-girl and daughter, a desperate Love, and a pretty Crime howling in the mud in the street.

R.L.

66—7   RUTS

To the right the summer dawn wakes the leaves and vapours and noises of this corner of the park, and the slopes to the left bear in their purple shadow the thousand rapid ruts of the wet road. A fairy cavalcade. Indeed: carts laden with animals in gilded wood, masts and multi-coloured canvas, drawn at the gallop by twenty piebald circus horses, and children and men on their amazing mounts; — twenty floats, embossed and bedecked with flags and flowers like old-fashioned carriages out of fairy-stories, full of children tricked out for a suburban pastorale. — Even coffins under midnight-black canopies sporting ebony plumes, trotting past at the pace of great blue and black mares.

R.L.

69   DAWN

I have embraced the summer dawn.

Nothing yet stirred on palace façades. The water was dead calm. The bivouacs of shadow did not leave the woodland road. I walked along, waking living warm breaths, and precious stones stared, and wings rose noiselessly.

The first undertaking was, on the track already filled with the sparkle of cool, wan light, a flower which told me its name.

I laughed at the fair-haired waterfall which became dishevelled among the pine-trees: at its silvery summit I recognised the goddess.

Then I lifted her veils one by one. On the drive, waving my arms about. Across the plain, where I told on her to the cock. In the city she fled among the bell-towers and domes, and running like a beggar over the marble quays, I chased her.

Above the road, near a laurel wood, I encircled her with her gathered veils, and I felt a little her huge body. Dawn and child tumbled to the foot of the wood.

When I awoke it was midday.

R.L.

74   BARBARIAN

Long after days and seasons, and people and places,

The flag of raw meat on the silk of seas and arctic flowers; (they don't exist.)

Recovered from the old fanfares for heroism — which still attack our heart and head — far from former assassins —

O! The flag of raw meat on the silk of seas and arctic flowers; (they don't exist.)

Favours!

Braziers, raining in squalls of frost, — Favours! — fires in the rain of gusts of diamonds hurled by the earthly heart eternally carbonised for us. — O world! —

(Far from the old retreats and the old flames, which you can hear and feel,)

The braziers and foam. Music, the veering of gulfs and clashing of icicles on the stars.

O Favours, O world, O music! And there, the shapes, sweats, hair and eyes, floating. And white tears boiling — O favours! — and a woman's voice reaching the depths of arctic volcanoes and grottoes.

The flag . . .

R.L.

78   I have stretched ropes from belfry to belfry; garlands from window to window; chains of gold from star to star, and I dance.

79—80
GENIUS

He is affection and the present, since he has made the house open to frothy winter and summer's murmurs, he who has purified food and drink, he who is the charm of fleeting places and the super-human delight of halts. He is affection and the future, the strength and love that, standing in rages and tedium, we see pass by in the stormy sky and the flags of ecstasy.

O his breaths, his heads, his races; the terrible alacrity of the perfection of forms and action.

O fecundity of the mind and immensity of the universe!

He has known all of us and has loved us all. Let us know, on this winter's night, from cape to cape, from the tumultuous pole to the castle, from the crowd to the beach, from looks to looks, with strengths and wearinesses, let us know how to hail him and see him, and send him away, and beneath the tides and high on the deserts of snow, how to follow his views, his breaths, his body, his day.

R.L.

80—1
DEPARTURE

Seen enough. The vision has been encountered in every air.

Had enough. The murmur of towns in the evening, and in the sunshine, and always.

Known enough. The halts of life. — O Murmurs and Visions! Departure in new affection and noises!

R.L.

89   I armed myself against justice.

    I fled. O sorceresses, o misery, o hate, it is to you that my treasure was entrusted!

    I succeeded in extinguishing in my mind all human hope. I pounced with the stealth of a wild beast on all joy, to strangle it.

    I summoned the executioners so that, as I died, I might bite the butts of their rifles. I summoned the plagues to choke me with sand and blood. Unhappiness was my god. I stretched myself out in the mud. I dried myself in the air of crime.

90   But, dear Satan, ... you who like in a writer the absence of descriptive or instructive talents, for you I tear out these few, hideous pages from my notebook of a damned soul.

92   To whom shall I hire myself? What beast must be worshipped? What holy image attacked? What hearts shall I break? What lie must I uphold? — In what blood wade?

93   In the towns, the mud suddenly seemed to me red and black, like a mirror when the lamp moves round in the next room, like a treasure in the forest! Good luck, I cried, and I saw a sea of flames and smoke in the sky; and, on the left and on the right, all riches blazing like a thousand million thunderbolts.

94   Not even a friend. I could see myself in front of an enraged crowd, facing the firing squad, weeping at their wretched failure to understand, and forgiving them! — Like Joan of Arc! — 'Priests, professors, lawyers, you are making a mistake by putting me in the hands of the law. I've never been one of these people; I have never been a Christian; I come from a line of men who would sing as they were tortured; I don't understand the law; I have no moral sense, I am a savage: you're making a mistake ...'

    Yes, my eyes are closed to your enlightenment. I am a beast, a nigger. But I can be saved. You are fake niggers, you maniacal, ferocious, miserly crowd. Trader, you're a nigger; judge, you're a nigger; general, you're a nigger; emperor, you old itch, you're a nigger.

                                                 R.L.

99   'You see that elegant young man going into the beautiful, calm house: his name is Duval, Dufour, Armand, Maurice, or goodness knows what! A woman has devoted her life to loving that wicked fool: she is dead, she is certainly a saint in heaven now.'

103—4   For a long time I prided myself on possessing every possible landscape, and found the celebrities of painting and modern poetry ridiculous.

    I loved absurd paintings, overdoors, stage sets, circus backcloths, inn signs, popular coloured prints; old-fashioned literature, church Latin, erotic books innocent of spelling, novels of our grandmothers' time, fairy-tales, little books for children, old operas, silly refrains, naive rhythms.

105   I became accustomed to simple hallucination: I saw quite plainly a mosque in place of a factory, a school of drummers composed of angels, carriages on roads in the sky, a drawing-room at the bottom of a lake; monsters, mysteries; the title of a vaudeville raised terrors in front of me.

Then I explained my magic sophisms with the hallucination of words!

I ended up by thinking that the disorder of my mind was sacred.

107   Bombard us with lumps of dried earth. Against the windows of splendid shops! into drawing-rooms! Make the town eat its own dust. Corrode waterspouts. Fill boudoirs with a burning powder of rubies . . .

107   Oh! the drunken gnat at the inn's urinal, in love with the borage, and dissolved by a sunbeam!

108   HUNGER

If I have a taste, it's for little more than earth and stones. I always feed on air, rock, coal, iron. My hungers, turn. Graze, hungers, on the meadow of sounds. Suck up gay poison from convolvulus. Eat the flints man breaks, old stones of churches, pebbles from the ancient floods, loaves scattered in grey valleys.

108   Let me sleep! let me boil on the altars of Solomon. The broth runs over rust, and mingles with the Cedron.

109   It is found again! — What? — Eternity. It's the sea mingled with the sun.

109–10   My health was threatened. Terror set in. I would fall asleep for several days on end, and, when I got up, carried on with the saddest dreams. I was ripe for death, and by a route full of dangers my weakness would lead me to the ends of the earth and of Cimmeria, the land of shades and whirlwinds.

I had to travel, to divert the spells crowding my brain. Over the sea, which I loved as if it should have cleansed me of some taint, I saw the consoling cross arise. I had been damned by the rainbow. Happiness was my fatality, my remorse, my worm: my life would always be too huge to be devoted to strength and beauty.

R.L.

110   O seasons, O castles! What soul is flawless? I have made the magic study of happiness, which no one escapes.

111   O purity! purity!

It is this moment of awakening that has given me the vision of purity! — Through the spirit one goes to God!

Shattering misfortune!

112   No! no! now I rebel against death! Work seems too trivial to my
pride: my betrayal to the world would be too brief a torture. At the
last moment, I would attack, right and left . . .

Then, — oh! — poor dear soul, wouldn't eternity be lost for us!

113   MORNING

Did I not *once* have an agreeable, heroic, fabulous youth to record
on gold-leaf — too much good fortune! Through what crime, through
what fault have I deserved my present weakness? You who claim
that animals sob with grief, that sick men despair, that the dead
have bad dreams, try to recount my fall and my sleep. For I can no
more explain myself than the beggar with his everlasting Paternosters and Ave Marias. *I no longer know how to speak!*

Yet today I believe I have finished the account of my hell. It really
was hell; the old one, whose doors were opened by the son of
man.

From the same desert, in the same night, my tired eyes always
wake to the silver star, always, without emotion on the part of the
Kings of life, the three Magi, heart, soul and mind. When shall we go
beyond shores and mountains to greet the birth of the new work,
new wisdom, the flight of tyrants and demons, the end of superstition, to worship — for the first time! — Christmas on earth!

The song of the heavens, the progress of nations! Slaves, let us not
curse life.

                                                          R.L.

116   Our boat raised high in the motionless mists turns towards the
port of poverty, the enormous city with its sky stained by fire and
mud.

116   Sometimes I see in the sky endless beaches covered with white
nations rejoicing. Above me, a great golden ship waves its multi-
coloured flags in the morning breezes.

117   I have created all festivals, all triumphs, all dramas. I have tried to
invent new flowers, new stars, new flesh, new languages. I believed
I had acquired supernatural powers. Well! I must bury my imagination and my memories! Fine fame as an artist and story-teller all
swept away!

I! I who called myself a seer or an angel, exempt from all morality, I am brought back to earth, with a duty to seek, and rugged reality to embrace! Peasant!

118   Meanwhile, this is the vigil. Let us receive every influx of strength
and real tenderness. And at dawn, armed with an ardent patience,
we shall enter the splendid cities.

Why was I talking of a friendly hand! One great advantage is
that I can laugh at old, false loves, and strike shame into those lying

couples, — I have seen the women's hell down there; — and I shall be free to *possess truth in one soul and one body*.

120—1   Received the Post-card and V's letter a week ago. To make everything simpler, I've told the Post Office to forward any letters it holds to me at home, so you can write to me here if there's nothing waiting for me *poste restante*. I shan't comment on the Loyola's latest indecencies, and I've nothing more to do on that front for the time being, as it appears that the second 'portion' of the '1874 class contingent' is going to be called up on the third of November next or coming: night in the barrack-room:

DREAM

We're hungry in barracks —
    It's true . ..
Smells, shells. A sapper:
    'I'm the gruyère!' —
Lefebvre: 'Keller!'
The sapper: 'I'm the Brie!' —
The soldiers cut on their bread:
    'That's life!
The sapper. —'I'm the Roquefort!
    — 'It'll be the death of us! . . .
    — I'm the gruyère
    And the Brie! . . . etc.

WALTZ

We've been brought together, Lefebvre and I, etc.

Such preoccupations allow only absorpshun. However kindly return, when poss, the 'Loyolas' that might roll up.

One small request: would you tell me brief and exactly — what the science 'bachot' consists of nowadays, the classic part, and maths etc. — Let me know the point that has to be reached in each section: maths, phys., chem., etc., and then the titles, pronto, (and how to get them) of the books used in your school; for ex. for this bachot unless it's different from university to university: anyway, from the teachers and students you know, get genned up on this point of view I'm giving you. I specially want exact things, as I'd need to buy the books shortly. Square — bashing and round bachot, you see, would give me two or three nice seasons! To hell with such 'dainty work'. Only be a good sort and let me know the bestest way to go about it.

Nothing, but nothing, here.

I like to think that old Wolfarse and the leeches full of patriotic French beans or otherwise don't divert you more than you need to be. At least it's not sheeting snow as it is here.

Yours 'to the limits of my little strength'.

Write:

A. Rimbaud.
31, rue Saint-Barthélemy,
Charleville (Ardennes) goes without saying.

P.S. 'Braided' letters get to the point where the 'Nemery' had given the Loyola's newspapers to a *copper* to deliver them to me!

R.L.

122   What awful thing are you telling me now? What's this about military service again? ... Well, it's perhaps my fate to become a *legless cripple*! And then, I imagine that the military administration might leave me in peace! ... the military administration is capable of putting a cripple in prison, if only in a hospital.

125   The road, barely six yards wide, is covered all along the right-hand side by a snow-fall some six feet high which is constantly thrusting on to the road a three-foot-deep barrier which has to be struggled through in a dreadful blizzard of sleet. Look! not a shadow above, below or around, although we are surrounded by enormous objects; no more road, precipices, gorge nor sky: nothing but whiteness to think of, touch, see or not see ...

R.L.

126   ONE LOT: A SINGLE TOOTH.
        ONE LOT: TWO TEETH.
        ONE LOT: THREE TEETH.
        ONE LOT: FOUR TEETH.
        ONE LOT: TWO TEETH.

Dear Sir,

May I enquire if I have left anything on account with you? I wish to change services today, from this one whose name I do not even know, but in any case to one run by Aphinar. These services exist everywhere, but I, helpless wretch, can find nothing, as the first dog you meet will confirm.

So let me know the cost of Aphinar's services to Suez. I am completely paralysed, and should therefore like to find a ship quickly. Tell me at what time I must be carried aboard ...

R.L.

128   Here's the fine outcome: I'm sitting down, and from time to time, I get up and hop a hundred steps on my crutches, and sit down again. I can hold nothing in my hands. When I'm walking, I can't turn my head away from my one foot and the ends of the crutches. My head and shoulders are bent forward, and you're rounded like a hunchback. You quake to see things and people moving around you, in case they knock you down and break your other leg. People sneer to see you hop. Back on your seat, your hands are flabby and your armpits sawn through, and you look like an idiot. Despair takes over again and you stay put like a complete invalid, blubbering and

waiting for night-time to bring its everlasting insomnia and a morning even sadder than the evening before, etc., etc. To be continued in our next.

R.L.

NOTES

Chapter 1. Introduction

1. R. Étiemble, *Le Mythe de Rimbaud*, vol. II, *Structure du mythe* (Paris, 1952), p. 444.

Chapter 2. A 'prologue' and early verse poems

1. In *Rimbaud notre prochain* (Paris, 1956), pp. 39–48, Suzanne Briet gives the text, with Rimbaud's spelling mistakes, and describes the exercise book in which it was written.
2. This probably refers not to flowers but to cigarettes, familiarly known as 'roses'. See under 'Tabac' in Larousse, *Grand dictionnaire universel du XIXᵉ siècle* (1866–76), vol. 14, p. 1362, where a statistical table shows that cigarettes in pink packets — 'enveloppes roses' — were made of superior tobacco, and were more expensive than the 'bleues' made of ordinary tobacco. Rimbaud may be playing on two meanings of 'roses' (the translation 'smoking pinks' changes the flower, but preserves the ambiguity) and on the reader's stock response to 'roses'.
3. This line displeased Rimbaud's teacher, Georges Izambard, who proposed one of his own: 'Et je sens des baisers qui me viennent aux lèvres.' According to him, this proved acceptable to his pupil, and most editors seem to have preferred it; but we have retained Rimbaud's original conclusion (see Georges Izambard, *Rimbaud tel que je l'ai connu* (Paris, 1946), pp. 41–2).
4. In a letter to Izambard (24 September 1870) Rimbaud's mother refers to her son as 'ce petit drôle'. In *Une Saison en enfer*, he himself sums up his relationship with Verlaine as a 'drôle de ménage', and in a letter from Aden (10 September 1884) he writes: 'C'est la vie: elle n'est pas drôle!'

Chapter 4. From poet to voyant

1. An earlier version of this poem, entitled 'Le Cœur supplicié', was sent to Izambard on 13 May 1871; the second version, sent to Demeny on 10 June 1871, with the title 'Le Cœur du pitre', is identical, except for punctuation and 'lance' instead of 'pousse' in l. 6. A third version, with several changes and a new title, 'Le Cœur volé', was copied out by Verlaine in October 1871, and discovered, it is believed, in 1898. It was first published in 1912. This is the version quoted here. The other two versions differ as follows: ll. 2 and 8, 'Mon cœur est *plein de* caporal'; 10 and 16, 'Leurs *insultes* l'ont dépravé!'; 11, '*À la vesprée ils font* des fresques'; 14,

'Prenez mon cœur, qu'il soit *sauvé*'; 19, 'Ce seront des *refrains* bachiques';
22, '*Si mon cœur* triste est ravalé'.

2. E. Delahaye, *Rimbaud, l'artiste et l'être moral* (Paris, 1923), p. 150.
3. Letter to Demeny (28 August 1871).
4. Most of these are discussed, and dismissed, by R. Étiemble in *Le Sonnet des Voyelles* (Paris, 1968).
5. For Verlaine's references to 'Voyelles', see Verlaine, *Œuvres en prose complètes* (Pléiade edition, Paris, 1972), pp. 643–56, 799–804.
6. G. Kahn, *Symbolistes et décadents* (Paris, 1902), pp. 248–50.
7. J.-P. Sartre, *Saint-Genet, comédien et martyr* (Paris, 1952), pp. 429–30.
8. S. Beckett, *Drunken Boat. A translation of Arthur Rimbaud's poem 'Le Bateau ivre'*, ed. with an introduction by J. Knowlson and F. Leakey (Reading, 1976), p. 33.
9. Despite inaccuracies, this book is useful, as it was one of the first to consider technical aspects of Rimbaud's poetry.

Chapter 5. Last and new verses

1. *L'Album zutique* (Paris, 1962). Photographic reproduction, with introduction and notes by Pascal Pia.
2. In a letter to Delahaye, Rimbaud quotes Musset's expression, 'Ô Nature! ô ma mère!', and includes amusing sketches with variants on it: 'Ô nature! ô ma sœur!' and 'O nature! ô ma tante!' (Reproduced in *Album Rimbaud* (Paris, 1967), p. 159).
3. Théodore de Banville, *Petit traité de poésie française* (Paris, 1871), pp. 56–7, 63.
4. Verlaine, *Œuvres en prose complètes*, pp. 655–6.

Chapter 6. *Illuminations*

1. For arguments in favour of the 'new order', see H. de Bouillane de Lacoste, *Rimbaud et le problème des 'Illuminations'* (Paris, 1949); and for the case against this view, and a convincing justification of the traditional order, consult C. Chadwick, *Études sur Rimbaud* (Paris, 1965), pp. 74–132.
2. Albert Camus, *Essais* (Pléiade edition, Paris, 1965), p. 497.
3. Apart from these five, the *Illuminations* were published, together with some of the 1872 verse poems, in the following numbers of *La Vogue*: no. 5 (13 May), no. 6 (29 May–3 June), no. 7 (7–14 June), no. 8 (13–20 June), no. 9 (21–27 June).
4. N. Wing, *Present Appearances: aspects of poetic structure in Rimbaud's 'Illuminations'* (University, Mississippi, 1974), p. 11.
5. During their time in London, Rimbaud and Verlaine saw paintings by Turner at the National Gallery, and in a letter to Émile Blémont (5 October 1872) Verlaine wrote: 'zut pour ce farceur de Turner: un mauvais Monticelli!'
6. These aspects are discussed in G. E. Evans and D. Thomson, *The Leaping Hare* (London, 1972). Numerous other references can be found: for example, W. B. Yeats, in 'The Celtic element in literature' (*Essays and Intro-*

ductions, London, 1961), pp. 178—9, associates the hare with a primaeval time: 'The hare that ran by among the dew might have sat up on his haunches when the first man was made . . .'; and Villiers de l'Isle-Adam, in *Tribulat Bonhomet* (Paris, 1967), p. 108, mentions a Canadian religion 'based on the belief that the universe was created by a great hare'.

7. See the *Lettre du voyant*: 'cet odieux génie qui a inspiré Rabelais, Voltaire, Jean La Fontaine, commenté par M. Taine!'; and compare the hare's morning prayer with Rimbaud's 'Oraison du soir'.

8. Rimbaud's references to spring are usually ironical, for instance, 'Et le printemps m'a apporté l'affreux rire de l'idiot', at the beginning of *Une Saison en enfer*. Valéry re-echoes this contempt for the return of the seasons and nature's vain attempts to create: 'Le retour des saisons et de leurs effets donne l'idée de la sottise de la nature et de la vie, laquelle ne sait que se répéter pour subsister' (*Traduction en vers des Bucoliques de Virgile, Œuvres*, Pléiade edition, Paris, 1957, vol. I, p. 208).

9. A. Barre, *Le Symbolisme. Essai historique sur le mouvement poétique en France de 1885 à 1900* (Paris, 1912), pp. 292—3. Barre fails to see that Rimbaud's 'simplicité' and 'ingénuité' constitute what Baudelaire termed a child-like 'perception' — 'une perception aiguë, magique à force d'ingénuité!'

10. M. Deguy, 'La Poésie en question', in *Modern Language Notes* (1970), pp. 421—2.

11. J. Gengoux, *La Pensée poétique de Rimbaud* (Paris, 1950), p. 514.

12. Rimbaud, *Œuvres complètes*, ed. A. Adam (Pléiade edition, Paris, 1972), p. 980.

13. A. R. Chisholm, review of C. A. Hackett, *Rimbaud* (London, 1957), in *AUMLA*, no. 8 (1958), p. 48.

14. *Arthur Rimbaud, 'Illuminations'*, ed. Albert Py (Geneva—Paris, 1967), p. 90.

15. A. Henry, 'Linguistique structurale et esthétique littéraire: un essai d'explication de "Enfance" de Rimbaud', in *Méthodes de la grammaire. Tradition et nouveauté* (Paris, 1966), p. 113.

16. Enid Starkie, *Arthur Rimbaud* (London, 1961), p. 169.

17. There are striking similarities between Rimbaud's town and the Coke-town of Dickens's *Hard Times*: streets 'all very like one another'; people 'equally like one another' and doing 'the same work'; every day 'the same as yesterday and tomorrow'; every year 'the counterpart of the last and the next'; everywhere 'soot and smoke' and, on a 'sunny midsummer day', shadows of mills and machines, Coketown's substitute for 'the shadows of rustling woods'. (Delahaye, in *Souvenirs familiers à propos de Rimbaud, Verlaine et Germain Nouveau* (Paris, 1925), p. 60, states that Rimbaud used to carry a translation of *Hard Times* in his pocket.) In a wider context, it is interesting to note Dickens's use in *Hard Times* of the words 'Fairy' and 'illumination' — the great factories are 'illuminated, like Fairy palaces' and (the opening sentence of chapter XI) 'The Fairy palaces burst into illumination . . .'.

18. V. P. Underwood, 'Reflets anglais dans l'œuvre de Rimbaud', in *Revue de littérature comparée*, 34° année (oct.—déc. 1960), pp. 547—8.

19. Some critics have taken 'front' to mean 'forehead'; others think that 'au front des palais' is an anglicism, 'in front of the palaces'. Littré, on the

other hand, gives: 'Étendue que présente le devant de certaines choses. Le front d'un bâtiment'; and it is in the sense of 'façade' that Du Bellay uses it when writing about the 'front audacieux' of the 'palais romains'.

20. The presence of this word has been taken as evidence that Rimbaud composed the poem after his visit to Stuttgart in 1875; but he did not need to go to Germany in order to become acquainted with the term 'wasserfall' — its strangeness and its sound make it more suitable in this context than 'chute d'eau' or 'cascade'.

21. W. M. Frohock, *Rimbaud's Poetic Practice* (Oxford, 1963), p. 192.

22. In many respects, both general and particular, 'Barbare' is reminiscent of passages in Empedocles's *The Nature of the Universe*, where human bodies are constantly being dismembered — with eyes, arms and heads 'floating' — and then reconstructed, as nature strives towards unity and harmony.

23. A sentence in Lorand Gaspar's poem, *Approche de la parole* (Paris, 1978), p. 137, could appropriately be quoted to sum up this interpretation of 'Barbare': 'Le monde établi dans sa douce, sa sauvage, sa cuisante fluidité. Inachevé et inachevable'.

24. J. Rivière, *Rimbaud* (new edition, Paris, 1938), p. 230.

25. See Roger Little, 'Rimbaud's "Mystique": some observations', *French Studies*, XXVI, no. 3 (July 1972), pp. 285—9, and '*Ut pictura poesis*: an element of order in the adventure of the *poème en prose*', in *Order and adventure in post-Romantic French poetry* (Oxford, 1973), pp. 244—56.

26. This term, in preference to *poème en prose*, is suggested by Saint-John Perse. See *Œuvres complètes* (Pléiade edition, Paris, 1972), pp. 518—19.

Chapter 7. *Une Saison en Enfer*

1. René Char's aphorism about his own dynamic spirit could be applied to the Rimbaud of *Illuminations*: 'Être du bond. N'être pas du festin, son épilogue' (*Feuillets d'Hypnos*).

2. E. Delahaye, *Les Illuminations et Une Saison en enfer* (Paris, 1927), p. 199.

3. G. Bachelard, *L'Eau et les rêves* (Paris, 1942), 132—3.

4. This quotation and the quotations in parentheses are from 'Poèmes de Verlaine inspirés par Rimbaud', in J. Mouquet, *Rimbaud raconté par Paul Verlaine* (Paris, 1934), pp. 211—41.

5. Paul Claudel, *Œuvres en prose* (Pléiade edition, Paris, 1965), pp. 37—8.

6. Monsieur Prudhomme is a character created by Henri Monnier. He represents the complacent, pompous bourgeois of the reign of Louis-Philippe. He first appeared briefly in *Scènes populaires, dessinées à la plume* (1830); and his philistine opinions and grandiloquent utterances are fully recorded in *Mémoires de Monsieur Joseph Prudhomme* (1857).

Chapter 8. Last poem and last letters

1. Paul Eluard, *Donner à voir* (Paris, 1938), pp. 139—40. Eluard also included 'Rêve' in his anthology, *Le Meilleur Choix de poèmes est celui que l'on fait pour soi. 1818—1918* (Paris, 1947), p. 128.

2. André Breton, *Manifestes du surréalisme* (Paris, 1962), p. 317.

3. Henri Michaux, *Ecuador* (Paris, 1929), p. 52.
4. See J. Réda's article in *aujourd'hui, Rimbaud . . .* (enquête de Roger Munier), *Archives des lettres modernes*, no. 160 (Paris, 1976), p. 107. For Rimbaud's letter dated 3 November 1887, see *Œuvres complètes* (Pléiade edition), p. 454.

Chapter 9. Conclusion

1. B. Fondane, *Rimbaud le voyou* (Paris, 1933), p. 22. New edition (Paris, 1979), p.28.
2. A recent, though distorted, example of Rimbaud's paradoxical role in religious conversions is found in John Tavener's opera, *Thérèse* (first performance 1 October 1979): 'Arthur Rimbaud,/Poet of sacrilege,/Who kicks the damned to God'. (See *Thérèse*, Libretto: Gerard McLarnon, Chester Music, 1979, p. 12; and letter from C. A. Hackett in *Opera*, vol. 31, no. 2 (February 1980), p. 201.)

CHRONOLOGICAL TABLE

Year	Life and Works	Contemporary events
1852		Napoleon III. Second Empire Hugo: *Napoléon le petit*
1853	8 February. Frédéric Rimbaud (Infantry Captain) marries Marie-Catherine-Vitalie Cuif 2 November. Jean-Nicolas-Frédéric Rimbaud born	Hugo: *Les Châtiments*
1854	20 October. Jean-Nicolas-Arthur Rimbaud born, Charleville	Crimean War Livingstone explores Central Africa and combats slave traffic Dickens: *Hard Times* (Fr. trans. 1857) Nerval: *Les Filles du feu, Les Chimères* Sainte-Beuve: *Les Lundis* (1849–69)
1855	Captain Rimbaud with French army in the Crimea	Fall of Sebastopol Paris Exhibition Sir Richard Burton, the first European, enters Harar Whitman: *Leaves of Grass*
1856		Congress of Paris Birth of the Prince Imperial Hugo: *Les Contemplations*
1857	4 April. Victorine-Pauline-Vitalie Rimbaud born; died July	Port of Dakar founded Burton explores sources of the Nile Banville: *Odes funambulesques* Baudelaire: *Les Fleurs du mal* Champfleury: *Le Réalisme* Flaubert: *Madame Bovary* Monnier: *Mémoires de Monsieur Joseph Prudhomme*
1858	15 June. Jeanne-Rosalie-Vitalie Rimbaud born	Orsini bomb attempt on life of Napoleon III

Year	Life and Works	Contemporary events
1859		War of Italian Unification. Magenta and Solferino Construction of Suez Canal begun Darwin: *The Origin of Species* (Fr. trans. 1862) Hugo: *La Légende des siècles* (1re série) Death of Marceline Desbordes-Valmore
1860	1 June. Frédérique-Marie-Isabelle Rimbaud born August. Captain and Madame Rimbaud separate	Garibaldi invades Sicily and Naples Baudelaire: *Les Paradis artificiels* Glatigny: *Les Vignes folles*
1861		Victor Emmanuel, first king of Italy Abraham Lincoln, President of U.S.A. American Civil War
1862	Rimbaud starts school at the Institution Rossat, Charleville	Annexation of Cochin-China Red Sea port of Obokh bought by a French commercial firm Baudelaire: publishes 20 *petits poèmes en prose* in *La Presse* Hugo: *Les Misérables* Leconte de Lisle: *Poèmes barbares* Michelet: *La Sorcière*
1863		Littré: *Dictionnaire de la langue française* begun Renan: *Vie de Jésus* Taine: *Histoire de la littérature anglaise* Verne: *Cinq semaines en ballon*
1864		Delvau: *Dictionnaire érotique moderne* Glatigny: *Les Flèches d'or* Michelet: *La Bible de l'humanité*
1865	Enters Collège de Charleville	Bernard: *Introduction à l'étude de la médecine expérimentale*

Year	Life and Works	Contemporary events
1865		Proudhon: *Du principe de l'art et de sa destination sociale*
1866	First Communion	Austro-Prussian War Transatlantic cable laid Coppée: *Le Reliquaire* Hugo: *Les Travailleurs de la mer* Larousse: *Grand dictionnaire universel du XIXe siècle* (1er vol.) Mérat: *Les Chimères* Sully-Prudhomme: *Les Épreuves* Verlaine: *Poèmes saturniens* *Le Parnasse contemporain* (1re série)
1867	Beginning of friendship with Ernest Delahaye at the Collège de Charleville	Banville: *Les Exilés* Marx: *Das Kapital* Judith Walter (Gautier): *Le Livre de jade* Death of Baudelaire
1868	Sends a 60-hexameter Ode in Latin to the Prince Imperial on the occasion of his first communion	Coppée: *Intimités* Gillet et Magne: *Nouvelle flore française* Louisa Siefert: *Les Rayons perdus*
1869	Prize-winning Latin verse compositions published in *Le Moniteur de l'enseignement secondaire*	Suez Canal opened Government of Ollivier Coppée: *Le Passant* Ducasse (Lautréamont): *Les Chants de Maldoror* Hugo: *L'Homme qui rit* Mérat: *L'Idole* Verlaine: *Fêtes galantes* Verne: *Vingt mille lieues sous les mers*
1870	Georges Izambard appointed at the Collège de Charleville; takes an interest in Rimbaud's work, and encourages him to read Rabelais, Hugo, Banville, etc. 24 May. Rimbaud sends 3 poems — 'Sensation', 'Ophélie', 'Credo in unam' ('Soleil et chair') — to Banville for publication in *Le Parnasse contemporain*	Franco-Prussian War Siege of Paris Battle of Sedan Fall of Second Empire Third Republic Demeny: *Les Glaneuses* Ducasse (Lautréamont): *Poésies* Taine: *De l'intelligence*

Year	Life and Works	Contemporary events
1870	August—October. Two flights from home, one to Paris, the other to Belgium. At Douai, copies out 22 of his poems, forming the 'recueil Demeny'	Verlaine: *La Bonne Chanson* (announced, but publication delayed until 1872)
	2 January. 'Les Étrennes des orphelins' published in *La Revue pour tous* 13 August. 'Trois Baisers' ('Première soirée') published in *La Charge*	
1871	End of February. Third 'flight' — to Paris 10 March. Returns to Charleville 13 May. Letter to Izambard formulating the *voyant* theory. 15 May. Letter to Demeny, generally known as the *Lettre du voyant* 10 June. Letter to Demeny ordering him to burn the poems given him in October 1870; sends him 'Les Poètes de sept ans', 'Les Pauvres à l'église', 'Le Cœur du pitre' 15 August. Letter to Banville, with 'Ce qu'on dit au poète à propos de fleurs' End August—early September. Letter to Verlaine, with 8 poems: 'Les Effarés', 'Accroupissements', 'Les Douaniers', 'Le Cœur volé', Les Assis', 'Mes petites amoureuses', 'Les Premières communions', 'Paris se repeuple' ?10 September. Leaves Charleville for Paris, on invitation from Verlaine, taking with him 'Le Bateau ivre'. Attends meetings of the Cercle zutique and the *Vilains Bonshommes*	1 January. Mézières and Charleville occupied by the Germans 28 January. Armistice signed February. Government of Thiers 18 March. Beginning of the Commune 21—28 May. The 'Semaine Sanglante' Banville: *Idylles prussiennes* Glatigny: *Le Fer rouge, Nouveaux châtiments* Renan: *La Réforme intellectuelle et morale* Zola: *La Fortune des Rougon* *Le Parnasse contemporain* (2e série)
1872	Late February. Returns to Charleville March. Works on poems, now included in *Vers nouveaux et chansons*	Military service made compulsory for all Frenchmen between ages of 20 and 40

Year	Life and Works	Contemporary events
1872	May. In Paris 7 July. With Verlaine in Belgium 7 September. With Verlaine in London, 34 Howland Street, W.1. Studies English, and frequents French exiles from the Commune (Andrieu, Régamey, Vermerch, etc.) November–December. Leaves Verlaine and returns to Charleville 14 September. 'Les Corbeaux' published in *La Renaissance littéraire et artistique*	International Exhibition, London Fantin-Latour: *Coin de table* (portraits of Verlaine and Rimbaud, with Léon Valade, Ernest d'Hervilly, Camille Pelletan, Pierre Elzéar Bonnier, Émile Blémont, Jean Aicard – and a vase of flowers in place of the 'voyant', Albert Mérat) Banville: *Petit traité de poésie française* Coppée: *Les Humbles* Hugo: *L'Année terrible* Taine: *Notes sur l'Angleterre*
1873	January–March. With Verlaine in London 25 March. Obtains a Reader's Ticket at the British Museum ?4 April. Returns to France with Verlaine 12 April. At Roche. Begins the 'Livre païen' or 'Livre nègre' 27 May. With Verlaine in London, 8 Great College Street, Camden Town, N.W.1 3 July. Quarrels with Verlaine, who goes to Brussels 8 July. Joins Verlaine in Brussels 10 July. Shot at and wounded by Verlaine (the so-called 'drame de Bruxelles') August. At Roche. Finishes the 'Livre païen', which becomes *Une Saison en enfer* October. Publication of *Une Saison en enfer* (Poot, Brussels)	Death of Napoleon III Corbière: *Les Amours jaunes* Cros: *Le Coffret de santal* Demeny: *Les Visions* Mérat: *Les Villes de marbre*
1874	March. With Germain Nouveau in London, 178 Stamford Street, S.E.1. Copies out some of the *Illuminations* 4 April. Obtains a Reader's Ticket at the British Museum	First Exhibition of Impressionist paintings, Paris Flaubert: *La Tentation de Saint-Antoine* Gautier: *Histoire du Romantisme*

Year	Life and Works	Contemporary events
1874	6 July. Joined in London by Madame Rimbaud and Vitalie November. At Reading, teaching French December. Returns to Charleville	Thomson: *The City of Dreadful Night* (serialised in the *National Reformer*) Verlaine: *Romances sans paroles*
1875	February—April. At Stuttgart; learns German; last meeting with Verlaine May—June. In Switzerland and Italy (Milan) July. In Paris October. At Charleville 14 October. Letter to Delahaye, containing 'Rêve' 12 December. Receives last letter from Verlaine; but does not reply	
1876	April. In Vienna May. In Holland. Enlists in the Dutch Foreign Legion 19 July. Arrives in Batavia, with units of the Dutch Foreign Legion 15 August. Deserts, and by December is back in Charleville	Invention of the telephone by Bell Mallarmé: *L'Après-midi d'un faune* *Le Parnasse contemporain* (3ᵉ série)
1877	May. In Bremen June. In Stockholm September. Back in Charleville	Invention of the phonograph by Edison and Cros Hugo: *La Légende des siècles* (2ᵉ série)
1878	Most of the year in the Ardennes; summer at Roche 20 October. Through the Vosges and Switzerland, and across the St Gotthard to Milan and Genoa 17 November. Captain Rimbaud dies at Dijon December. Rimbaud works in Cyprus for the firm of E. Jean et Thial fils, as foreman of a quarry gang 'Petits Pauvres' ('Les Effarés') published in *The Gentleman's Magazine*, London	Congress of Berlin
1879	Ill with typhoid; leaves Cyprus and returns to Roche for the summer and winter. Visited by Delahaye	Death of the Prince Imperial Vallès: *Jacques Vingtras* (1879—86)

Year	Life and Works	Contemporary events
1880	March—July. In Cyprus, helping to build the summer residence of the British Governor-General, on Mount Troodos 20 July. Seeks work at Alexandria, then at ports along the Red Sea 7 August. In Aden, employed by Mazeran, Viannay, Bardey and Co., traders in coffee, skins, etc. December. In Abyssinia, at the firm's branch office in Harar	
1881	May—June. Expedition to Bubassa for ivory December. Leaves Harar and returns to Aden	French Protectorate over Tunisia Ministry of Gambetta Flaubert: *Bouvard et Pécuchet* Verlaine: *Sagesse*
1882	In Aden	The British occupy Cairo Champsaur: *Dinah Samuel* (Rimbaud appears as Arthur Cimber, 'le plus grand poète de la terre', and an extract from 'Les Chercheuses de poux' is quoted)
1883	March. Returns to Harar. Report on Sotiro's expedition into the Ogaden sent to the Société de Géographie, Paris (published, 1884)	Verlaine: *Les Poètes maudits* in the review *Lutèce* (in volume form, 1884) — includes a study of Rimbaud, and quotes 6 verse poems
1884	Harar office closes. March. Leaves for Aden and signs new contract with his firm, now Bardey frères	Huysmans: *À rebours* Verlaine: *Jadis et naguère*
1885	October. Leaves Bardey frères to traffic in arms	Beauclair et Vicaire: *Les Déliquescences d'André Floupette* (contains a parody of 'Oraison du soir') Laforgue: *Les Complaintes* Mallarmé: *Prose pour des Esseintes* Death of Hugo
1886	October. Starts from Tajoura for Ankober with a caravan of rifles and cartridges for Menelik, King of Shoa	Bloy: *Le Désespéré* Conversion of Claudel

Year	Life and Works	Contemporary events
1886	Les Illuminations (sic) published in 5 nos. of La Vogue: and in volume form, with a preface by Verlaine. Une Saison en enfer appears later, in 3 nos. of the review	
1887	6 February. In Ankober April. Reaches Entoto (Addis Ababa) and delivers arms to Menelik. Meets the Swiss engineer, Alfred Ilg, the King's technical adviser 7 May. Leaves for Harar with the explorer Borelli 30 July. In Aden 20 August. In Cairo with his native servant Djami 25 August. Article on Abyssinia published in Le Bosphore Égyptien. Sends articles to newspapers in France October. In Aden December. Writes to French government for authorisation to build an arms factory in Shoa	Dujardin: Les Lauriers sont coupés Kahn: Les Palais nomades
1888	Engaged in gun-running on behalf of Armand Savouré until mid-May, when he gives up arms traffic, and enters into partnership with César Tian. Opens a trading station at Harar	Plowert (Adam): Petit glossaire pour servir à l'intelligence des auteurs décadents et symbolistes Verlaine: Amour
1889	In touch with Mgr Taurin-Cahagne, Bishop of Harar, and André Jarosseau, of the Catholic mission at Harar 20 December. Writes to Ilg asking for a mule and two slaves	Paris Exhibition (Centenary of the French Revolution) New law reducing period of military service Menelik becomes Emperor of Abyssinia Verlaine: Parallèlement
1890	Receives letter dated 17 July, from Laurent de Gavoty, director of La France moderne, asking him to collaborate as 'chef de l'école décadente et symboliste'. Does not reply	

Year	Life and Works	Contemporary events
1891	April. Forced by illness to leave Abyssinia 20 May. Hôpital de la Conception, Marseilles 27 May. Right leg amputated 23 July. Goes to Roche 23 August. Returns with Isabelle to hospital, Marseilles, where he dies, 10 November. Buried at Charleville *Arthur Rimbaud. Reliquaire. Poésies* (with preface by Rodolphe Darzens) *Arthur Rimbaud. Poèmes. Les Illuminations. Une Saison en enfer* (with preface by Paul Verlaine)	Laforgue: 'Notes sur Baudelaire, Corbière, Mallarmé, Rimbaud', in *Entretiens politiques et littéraires* Moore: 'Two Unknown Poets' (Laforgue and Rimbaud), in *Impressions and Opinions*

SELECT BIBLIOGRAPHY

Editions

Œuvres complètes, ed. R. de Renéville and J. Mouquet, 'Bibliothèque de la Pléiade', Paris, 1946; new editions, 1954 and 1963.

Œuvres, ed. Suzanne Bernard, Paris, 1960; new edition, 1962.

Œuvres complètes, ed. A. Adam, 'Bibliothèque de la Plèiade; Paris, 1972.

Poésies, édition critique, introduction et notes par H. de Bouillane de Lacoste, Paris, 1939; new edition, 1947.

Poésies, édition critique, introduction, classement chronologique et notes par M. A. Ruff, Paris, 1978.

Illuminations, édition critique, avec introduction et notes par H. de Bouillane de Lacoste, Paris, 1949.

Illuminations, texte établi, annoté et commenté avec une introduction, un répertoire des thèmes et une bibliographie, par A. Py, Geneva–Paris, 1967.

Illuminations, ed. N. Osmond, London, 1976.

Une Saison en enfer, édition critique, introduction et notes par H. de Bouillane de Lacoste, Paris, 1941; new edition, 1943.

Lettres du voyant, éditées et commentées par G. Schaeffer. *La Voyance avant Rimbaud*, par M. Eigeldinger, Geneva–Paris, 1975.

Critical studies

Books

Rivière, J. *Rimbaud*, Paris, 1930; new edition, 1938.

Étiemble, R. and Gauclère, Y. *Rimbaud*, Paris, 1936; new edition, 1950.

Starkie, Enid. *Arthur Rimbaud*, London, 1938; new editions, 1947 and 1961.

Chadwick, C. *Études sur Rimbaud*, Paris, 1960.

Bonnefoy, Y. *Rimbaud par lui-même*, Paris, 1961.

Frohock, W. M. *Rimbaud's Poetic Practice*, Harvard University Press, 1963.

Houston, J. P. *The Design of Rimbaud's Poetry*, Yale University Press, 1963.

Hackett, C. A. *Autour de Rimbaud*, Paris, 1967.

Plessen, J. *Promenade et Poésie. L'expérience de la marche et du mouvement dans l'œuvre de Rimbaud*, The Hague and Paris, 1967.

Davies, Margaret. *Une Saison en enfer, analyse du texte*, Paris, 1975.

Kittang, A. *Discours et jeu: Essai d'analyse des textes d'Arthur Rimbaud*, Oslo and Grenoble, 1975.

Articles

Scarfe, F. 'A stylistic interpretation of Rimbaud', *Archivum Linguisticum*, vol. III, fasc. II (1951), pp. 166–92.

Richard, J.-P. 'Rimbaud ou la poésie du devenir', in *Poésie et profondeur* (Paris, 1955), pp. 187–250.

Bernard, Suzanne. 'Rimbaud et la création d'une nouvelle langue poétique', in *Le Poème en prose de Baudelaire jusqu'à nos jours* (Paris, 1959), pp. 151–211.

Baudry, J.-L. 'Le texte de Rimbaud', *Tel Quel*, no. 35 (automne 1968), pp. 46–63; and 'Le texte de Rimbaud' (fin), *Tel Quel*, no. 36 (hiver 1969), pp. 33–53.

Chambers, R. 'Rimbaud et le regard créateur', *Saggi e ricerche di letteratura francese* (Pisa), vol. X (1969), pp. 199–228.

Lawler, J. R. 'Rimbaud as Rhetorician', in *The Language of French Symbolism* (Princeton University Press, 1969), pp. 71–111.

Little, R. 'Rimbaud: au seuil de l'illumination', in *Revue des Lettres Modernes: Arthur Rimbaud*, vol. II (Paris, 1973), pp. 81–105.

Freadman, Anne. 'To read Rimbaud (b) A reading of "Mystique"', *Australian Journal of French Studies*, vol. XI, no. I, (1974), pp. 65–82.

Guyaux, A. 'À propos des *Illuminations*: Note sur le mot illisible de "Villes"', and 'Y a-t-il des textes sans titre dans les *Illuminations?*', *Revue d'histoire littéraire de la France*, 77° année, no. 5 Sept.–Oct. 1977), pp. 795–811.

Todorov, T. 'Une complication de texte: les *Illuminations*', *Poétique*, no. 34 (avril 1978), pp. 241–53.

Roubaud, J. '"Ce n'est rien! j'y suis! j'y suis toujours"', in *La Vieillesse d'Alexandre* (Paris, 1978), pp. 19–35.

Translations (with the original text)

A Season in Hell and *The Drunken Boat*, English translation by Louise Varèse, New York, 1945.

Prose Poems from the Illuminations, in a new translation by Louise Varèse, New York, 1946.

A Season in Hell. The Illuminations, a new translation by Enid Rhodes Peschel; Foreword by Henri Peyre, Oxford, 1973.

For important documentary material and biographical details, see Matarasso, H., and Petitfils, P., *Album Rimbaud*, Paris, 1967; and, for bibliographical material, Petitfils, P., *L'Œuvre et le visage d'Arthur Rimbaud: essai de bibliographie et d'iconographie*, Paris, 1949; Etiemble, R., *Le Mythe de Rimbaud: I. Genèse du mythe*, Paris, 1954, II. *Structure du mythe*, 1952, *L'Année du centenaire*, 1961; and Bernard, Suzanne, 'État présent des études sur Rimbaud', in *L'Information littéraire*, nos. 2–3, 1962. See also three reviews devoted to Rimbaud studies; *Études rimbaldiennes* (Paris, 1967–72); *Revue des Lettres Modernes; Arthur Rimbaud* (Paris, 1972–); and *Rimbaud vivant. Bulletin des Amis de Rimbaud* (1973–).

INDEX